TRAFFIC

SCREENPLAY BY
STEPHEN GAGHAN

INTRODUCTION BY
STEVEN SODERBERGH
AND STEPHEN GAGHAN

faber and faber

First Edition
First published in the United States in 2001
by Newmarket Press, 18 East 48 Street, New York, NY 10017

First published in the United Kingdom in 2001
by Faber and Faber Limited
3 Queen Square London WC1N 3AU

Printed and bound in Great Britain by
Mackays of Chatham plc, Chatham, Kent

The right of STEPHEN GAGHAN to be identified as author of this
work has been asserted in accordance with Section 77 of the
Copyright, Designs and Patents Act 1988.

A CIP record for this book
is available from the British Library.

ISBN 0-571-21270-0

2 4 6 8 10 9 7 5 3 1

FADE IN:

1   EXT. COLUMBUS, OHIO - DAY   1

The state capital of Ohio. It's an impressive building for a
city this size.

SUPERTITLE: COLUMBUS, OHIO - STATE CAPITAL

2   INT. OHIO STATE SUPREME COURT - DAY   2

In chambers striving for august, JUSTICES listen to a lawyer,
MR. RODMAN, argue his case before the highest court in Ohio.
Mr. Rodman enjoys the sound of his own voice.

> MR. RODMAN
> This informant, paid by the police, using
> taxpayer dollars to continue his felony
> drug habit, was the link which allowed
> police to raid a private farm. A working
> farm. A farm where honest Americans make
> their living.

One particular justice, ROBERT WAKEFIELD, younger than the
others, is clearly bemused by this performance.

> MR. RODMAN (CONT'D)
> The government, in its haste, has
> employed an army of criminals whose
> allegiance to the truth is, at best,
> questionable --

Judge Wakefield interrupts --

> ROBERT
> Mr. Rodman...it's too bad your client
> didn't show as much sense in choosing
> what he planted as he did in choosing his
> attorney...

A polite chuckle from the justices --

> ROBERT (cont'd)
> Lately the only variation I'm hearing in
> your argument is the name of the client.
> And you can sit there all day arguing the
> ins and outs of *Illinois v. Gates*, but
> you aren't going to convince me that this
> country has not sanctioned the use of
> anonymous informants.
>   (beat)
> Furthermore, there is no sacred
> protection of property rights in the
> United States.
>   (MORE)

(CONTINUED)

                         ROBERT (cont'd)
               When you make the decision to have
               marijuana on your farm, whether it's one
               joint or an acre of plants, your property
               can be seized and your property can be
               sold.

                         MR. RODMAN
               I'm sorry the court finds my argument
               repetitious.

                         ROBERT
               Mr. Rodman, may I offer a piece of
               advice? The next time you argue this
               point before this court, regardless of my
               whereabouts, I recommend you have
               something up your sleeve other than your
               arm.

3   INT. ROBERT'S CHAMBERS - DAY   3

     The office is marble and dark wood. A young CLERK, black, 29,
     enters carrying an oddly-shaped gift. They both look at it.

                         CLERK
               What do you think it is?

                         ROBERT
               Depends who it's from.

                         CLERK
                    (reading the card)
               Your friends at Warren, Putnam and
               Hudson.

                         ROBERT
               You can learn a lot about somebody from
               this stuff. Three categories: you like
               me, you hate me, you want something from
               me.
                    (re: the elaborate box)
               Definitely third category.

                         CLERK
               What would a law firm want from the new
               drug Czar?

                         ROBERT
               Depends on the state.

                         CLERK
                    (checks)
               Arizona.

                                                      (CONTINUED)

3   CONTINUED: 3

                          ROBERT
                Medicinal marijuana initiative.
                     (beat)
                Or am I being cynical?

     They both laugh. Robert reaches up and pulls a bottle of
     Scotch from a shelf. He pours a couple of fingers in two
     glasses.

                          CLERK
                Maybe there's a book in it.

     The clerk takes one of the glasses.

                          ROBERT
                Not by me.

     They toast and drink.

A4   EXT. COURTHOUSE - DAY   A4

     Robert exits, trailed by a small group of reporters. He gets
     into a car being driven by two security TYPES.

4   INT. AIRPLANE - DAY   4

     Robert sits in a business class window seat.

5   INT. HOTEL ROOM - NIGHT   5

     An expensive hotel. Robert Wakefield stands at the window,
     looking at the view of our nation's capital.

     SUPERTITLE: WASHINGTON D.C.

     ON THE TABLE

     the remnants of a meal. It was a steak and a small caesar
     salad. The wine glass is half-empty.

     ANOTHER ANGLE ON ROBERT

     in front of the mirror now, trying on a dark, tasteful
     jacket.

6   CLOSER   6

     On Robert in the same position, only now we are in HIS HOME.
     It's daytime, and his wife BARBARA is helping him into this
     same jacket. As her hands dust the lint off his shoulders we
     MATCH CUT TO:

7   ROBERT   7

in the hotel room, making the same motions. Satisfied, he straightens, then turns to look at himself.

8   OMITTED   8

9   ANGLE ON ROBERT   9

back at the hotel room window now. Reaches to the table and lifts the wine glass.

          CUT TO:

10   EXT. DIRT ROAD - DAY   10

This is the middle of nowhere. Scrub cactus and dust and a heartless sun.

SUPERTITLE: MEXICO - TWENTY MILES SOUTHWEST OF TIJUANA.

A broken down-looking Police Sedan is parked on the side of the road. It seems abandoned except there are TWO MEN inside.

11   INT. POLICE SEDAN - DAY   11

Two Mexican men, State Police officers, JAVIER RODRIGUEZ, 30's, and MANUEL "MANOLO" SANCHEZ, 20's, wearing jeans, knock-off Polo shirts, and cowboy boots, wait patiently in the car.

          JAVIER
      I had that dream again.

A long pause.

          MANOLO
      Which one?

Another long pause.

          JAVIER
      Where my mother's suffocating.

They continue to wait until there is the sound of a JET ENGINE. It grows LOUDER as it approaches.

12   EXT. THE POLICE SEDAN - DAY   12

The shadow of a large plane crosses the desert floor. Then, an old DC-3 flies fifty feet above the Police Sedan.

13   INT. POLICE SEDAN - DAY   13

They watch the plane disappear over a small rise in the
desert. They look at each other and wait some more.

14   EXT. MEXICAN DESERT - LATER   14

From the direction of the landing strip, a moving van lumbers
down the road, two TEENAGERS in the cab.

15   INT. POLICE SEDAN - DAY   15

Javi and Manolo watch the moving van approach. Javi reaches
under the seat and picks up a bubble flasher. He rolls down
the window and plants it on the roof. He flips the switch.
Nothing happens. He jiggles the wire and the siren BURPS and
the light flashes. Manolo and Javi step from the car,
smiling.

16   EXT. MEXICAN DESERT - DAY   16

The moving van slows to a stop. Javi approaches. The DRIVER
unhurriedly rolls down the window.

                    DRIVER
          Is there a problem?

                    JAVIER
          No. There's no problem.

The driver hesitates a confused beat then reaches for his
wallet.

                    DRIVER
          Okay. I see. How much do you want?

The driver pulls a wad of bills. Javi shakes his head.

                    DRIVER (cont'd)
          You want more than this?

Javi shakes his head. The driver exchanges a look with his
partner.

                    DRIVER (cont'd)
          You want something else?

Javi smiles. The driver gets out and walks to the back of the
truck. He opens the rear door. There are neatly-stacked
crates marked with a SCORPION logo and "**911**." He reaches into
one of them and pulls out a tightly-sealed package also with
the scorpion stamped on it. He turns to see Javi with his gun
drawn.

                    (CONTINUED)

Manolo, at the passenger side, has also drawn his gun and is
motioning the partner to move to the back of the truck.

>   JAVIER
>   Drop the package. Put your hands behind
>   your head. You're under arrest.

The driver hesitates. He starts to comply then looks at Javi
and Manolo.

>   DRIVER
>   I don't understand. I think there must be
>   some mistake.

>   JAVIER
>   No, there's no mistake.

Javi motions to Manolo who cuffs both teenagers. The driver
begins spewing OBSCENITIES under his breath. Javi puts the
driver in the front of the Shadow. Manolo follows in the
moving van.

17   OMITTED   17

18   OMITTED   18

19   EXT. DIRT ROAD - MEXICO - LATER   19

The truck follows the Shadow down a desert road.

Suddenly, from behind, four armored SUV's with tinted windows
appear, closing fast.

The SUV's force both vehicles off the road where they pull to
a stop. A long beat as hot wind blows desert detritus past
the truck.

Finally, the SUV doors open and FEDERAL POLICE OFFICERS
surround them like a SWAT team.

The passenger door of the lead SUV opens and GENERAL ARTURO
SALAZAR, 50's, a squat, powerful presence in a perfectly
pressed uniform gets out and approaches Javi.

>   SALAZAR
>   (to Javier)
>   What's your name?

>   JAVIER
>   Javier Rodriguez.

                    SALAZAR
          Well, Javier Rodriguez, you've done a
          very good job, but we'll take care of it
          from here.

Javier stares into the implacable reflection of his
sunglasses. In the distance, the DC-3 takes off and ROARS
over their heads.

                    SALAZAR (cont'd)
          We've been following these Narco-
          trafficantes for some time but had not
          been able to bring them to justice.
               (to his men)
          Put the prisoners in the car. Impound the
          truck.

The men follow Salazar's orders.

                    SALAZAR (cont'd)
               (to Javi)
          One question. How did you find about
          this?

                    JAVIER
          An informant.

                    SALAZAR
          What is the name of your informant?

                    JAVIER
               (beat)
          It was an anonymous tip.

Salazar looks at Javi a beat.

                    SALAZAR
               (to his men)
          For a State Police officer, you're very
          well informed. Let's go.

MOMENTS LATER

Javi and Manolo watch the convoy of vehicles drive away.
Javier lights a cigarette.

                    MANOLO
          Wasn't that General Salazar?

                    JAVIER
          Yeah.

                                          (CONTINUED)

>   MANOLO
>   What's he doing up here?
>
>   JAVIER
>   I don't know. Something.

They start for their car.

20   OMITTED   20

21   OMITTED   21

22   OMITTED   22

23   EXT. DEL MAR SELF-STORAGE - DAY   23

SUPERTITLE: SAN DIEGO

Two men, RAY CASTRO, 30's, proud, ambitious, and MONTEL
GORDON, 40's, suspicious of everyone including himself and
always, always the smartest guy in the room, walk from a
Lincoln Towncar toward a dumpy office. Castro is talking
under his breath --

>   CASTRO
>   No telltales. Nothing to read. Not
>   touching my face. Not even blinking. No
>   giveaways.
>   (beat)
>   How're you feeling?
>
>   GORDON
>   (keyed up)
>   I feel good.
>
>   CASTRO
>   No more pissant basin league bullshit for
>   us, hunh?
>
>   GORDON
>   Nope.

Castro stretches his arms, swings them around.

>   CASTRO
>   Limbering up, gonna stay loose, keep it
>   all together. Take this motherfucker
>   down.

They reach the door to the office. Gordon looks at Castro,
then turns the handle.

                                                          (CONTINUED)

23   CONTINUED: 23

                    CASTRO (CONT'D)
              Showtime.

24   INT. OFFICE, DEL MAR SELF-STORAGE - DAY   24

      It's a cluttered, rundown working office unusual only in the
      extent of its ordinariness. A SECRETARY goes about her
      business like a somnambulist. CLERKS shuffle and file.

      Castro switches into Spanish --

                    CASTRO
                  (in Spanish)
              Good afternoon, ladies, gentlemen. We're
              looking for Eduardo Ruiz. We have a two
              o'clock appointment.

25   INT. OFFICE, DEL MAR SELF-STORAGE - LATER   25

      In a back alcove, Castro and Gordon sit across a cheap table
      from EDUARDO RUIZ, 40's, an entrepreneur in an expensive suit
      and bad hairpiece. They are waiting.

                    RUIZ
              You ever buy a quarter ton? Not many
              people have.

      Another "businessman" enters from another door and whispers
      in Ruiz's ear, then leaves again.

                    RUIZ (cont'd)
              So, it's worth the wait, right? What can
              I do? Rent a Huey? Have an airlift? It's
              not like you can put it in a condom up
              some mule's asshole, right? How many
              peasants would that take? A line
              stretching from here to Mexico City --

                    GORDON
              Nobody said shit, Eduardo --

      One of Ruiz's hands dips under the desk where we see a
      handgun is holstered on the underside.

                    RUIZ
              Relax. We're waiting, that's it.

                    CASTRO
              Hey, you want to hear a joke? I got a
              joke. Why do women wear makeup and
              perfume?

                                              (CONTINUED)

                         GORDON
               Chill out --

                         CASTRO
               It's a funny fuckin' joke and it's quick.
               Why do women wear makeup and perfume?

                         RUIZ
               I don't know.

                         CASTRO
               'Cause they're ugly and they stink.

Castro laughs uproariously.

26   INT. DEA SURVEILLANCE SPACE - DAY   26

ON FUZZY SURVEILLANCE VIDEO: Castro laughing. Ruiz politely
smiling, one of his hands hidden by the table.

                         GORDON
               Man, you never been close enough to a
               woman to know how she smells.

                         DEA AGENT (V.O.)
               What's his hand doing? Watch his hand.
               Anybody? I don't like the hand.

27   IN THE OFFICE   27

The room is filled with crappy surveillance equipment. DEA
AGENTS, in DEA logo'd outerwear, jiggle a monitor fuzzily
displaying the view from another hidden camera: Gordon and
Ruiz around the cheap table.

                         DEA AGENT
               This is ridiculous this fucking thing.
                    (taps monitor)
               Look at this shit -- the first television
               transmission. I had better shit when I
               was the AV guy at junior high, swear-to-
               God.

                         ANOTHER DEA AGENT
               Come on, Castro, pay attention. Watch his
               damn hands.

ON THE MONITOR

Another "businessman" enters the office and whispers in
Ruiz's ear.

                                                        (CONTINUED)

27   CONTINUED: 27

                         RUIZ (ON MONITOR)
              Soon.

     Another AGENT peers out a window through binoculars. HIS POV:
     the exterior of the office where Castro, Gordon, and Ruiz
     talk.

28   EXT. DEL MAR SELF-STORAGE, SAN DIEGO - DAY   28

     A BLUE VAN makes a slow turn into the parking lot.

29   EXT. ROOF - DAY   29

     TWO FBI AGENTS, in jackets reading "FBI," hide on an opposing
     roof. They look through high-powered binoculars. Binocular
     POV: the BLUE VAN turning into the plaza.

                         FBI AGENT #2
              All right, here we go. The blue van.

     His binocular POV detects three unmarked cars discreetly
     following the van.

                         FBI AGENT #2 (cont'd)
              Three unmarked vehicles.
                   (picks up walkie)
              Three unmarked vehicles accompanying.

     The unmarked cars split up and one turns into the parking lot
     of a fast-food restaurant. The other circles around the back
     of a building.

                         FBI AGENT #2 (CONT'D)
              It's local. Local or Customs. Oh, man, I
              don't know. Looks like the cavalry.

                         FBI AGENT
              This is our show. Ah, man. I don't want
              to share this one.

30   INT. OFFICE, DEL MAR SELF-STORAGE - CONTINUOUS   30

     Through the window Ruiz, Gordon and Castro watch the van
     disappear into the bay of a storage unit. A man is pulling
     down the door behind it when three unmarked squad cars ROAR
     into the lot, surrounding the unit, officers exit the cars
     with their guns drawn --

     Gordon and Castro stare in disbelief.

     Ruiz FIRES the gun under the desk which hits Gordon full in
     the chest, knocking him backwards.

                                              (CONTINUED)

Ruiz's men run into the room pulling guns.

Castro dives and pulls his weapon, firing at Ruiz's men,
hitting both of them. Ruiz bolts through another door. Castro
pursues, talking into his shirt collar --

                         CASTRO
              Agent down. Repeat, agent down.

Gordon gets slowly to his feet, shaking off the blast to his
Kevlar, and runs after them.

31   EXT. DEL MAR SELF-STORAGE - DAY   31

The DEA are shooting at the men inside the storage unit who
are shooting back.

From all over the stake-out location, DEA AGENTS emerge
firing their weapons. An equal number of FBI AGENTS emerge
firing in return. Nobody was aware of the other's presence.

It's CHAOS, a clusterfuck of law-enforcement zeal with three
competing sets of good guys shouting through BULL-HORNS,
GUNSHOTS and SCREAMING.

Ruiz breaks through the corner of the lot, cutting between
two buildings. Castro emerges and chases him.

32   EXT. PARKING LOT - DAY   32

Ruiz runs out the back of the storage company. He cuts
between parked cars, heading for The Fun Zone, a kiddie
restaurant.

33   INT. THE FUN ZONE - DAY   33

Castro enters The Fun Zone. There's a cardboard cutout of
SPASTIC JACK, a beloved comedy figure who looks like a rabbit
version of Jar Jar Binks, promoting the "Special Edition"
glass: "Collect All Four." There's an enclosure filled with
colored plastic balls.

The restaurant is empty except for a CLOWN filling out a time
card. The clown stands.

                         CLOWN
              Hey dudes, we're not open yet.

Castro makes a motion for him to be quiet and keeps moving
toward the room of colored balls.

Gordon enters the restaurant and follows him. An ANIMATRONIC
BAND starts to play a SONG.

                                                    (CONTINUED)

33   CONTINUED: 33

        Gordon sees a half-hidden foot buried underneath the plastic
        balls at the far end of the room. He takes careful aim and
        FIRES.

        Ruiz SCREAMS and sits up. Castro pounces on him, disarming
        him, and roughing him up.

34   EXT. THE FUN ZONE - DAY   34

        Castro and Gordon shove Ruiz into the sunlight. They wait
        while their eyes adjust.

                            RUIZ
                  Take me to the hospital. I'm bleeding to
                  death.

        Castro shoves him forward.

A35   ACROSS THE PARKING LOT   A35

        DEA has opened the back of the van where a quarter ton of
        cocaine is spilling out onto the pavement.

                                                        CUT TO:

35   INT. GUEST HOUSE - AFTERNOON   35

        A bong hit is expelled into the air. In the living room of a
        comfortable, preppy guest house, private school TEENAGERS
        party and hang-out: cigarettes in ashtrays, beer and bong on
        the coffee table, loud MUSIC.

        SUPERTITLE: CINCINNATI, OHIO

        The TV is on with the sound off. The curtains are closed.
        The four boys wear school blazers with their ties pulled
        askew, the three girls' clothing are also identical. Some sit
        on couches, some on the floor. They are stoned.

        One intense-looking boy, SETH ABRAHMS, 17, wild curly hair
        and the attitude of a young Coleridge, and a girl, CAROLINE
        WAKEFIELD, 16, really sixteen which means she looks about 12,
        pretty and flirtatiously irreverent, sit at a desk in front
        of a Powerbook G-3 playing an on-line trivia game. Seth
        speaks rapidly and precisely.

                            SETH
                  Father of Greek tragedy? Anyone? Okay,
                  Aeschylus it is.
                            (hits keys)
                  His trilogy? The Oresteia. I mean this is
                  beautiful, can anyone stop the Seth
                  Machine?
                            (MORE)

                                                   (CONTINUED)

                              SETH   (cont'd)
                         (hits keys)
                    Score. Thank you. Madmax from Omaha we
                    own you. And Tragedy is closed out.

Seth leans over and snorts a line of coke from a mirror. He
hands it to Caroline who effortlessly does one.

                              CAROLINE
                    Entertainment. The Susan Lucci section or
                    Banal Love Songs of the Nineties?

Seth looks at her. He has a crush.

                              SETH
                    Banal Love Songs it is.
                         (hits keys)
                    Hey, you wanna try something?

She nods. They both take a swig of beer. He takes her hand
pulling her past the stoned people on the couch --

IN THE KITCHEN

Seth takes out a box of baking soda. He tears off a square of
aluminum foil. He takes out a spoon. Caroline watches as he
dumps a small amount of cocaine into the spoon. He adds a
pinch of baking soda. He puts in a few drops of water. Stirs
it around with the heel of a lighter. Then holds the flame
under the spoon.

                              CAROLINE
                    What are you doing?

                              SETH
                         (concentrating)
                    Just watch.

He watches the substance in the spoon as it swirls and
bubbles, then separates... He pours the most viscous part
onto the aluminum foil, making four separate little puddles.

He quickly dismantles a ballpoint pen, making a straw. He
hands it to Caroline.

                              SETH (cont'd)
                    Inhale the smoke and hold it.

                              CAROLINE
                    What is this, like freebase?

                              SETH
                    Not like. It is.

                                                        (CONTINUED)

35   CONTINUED: (2)   35

He lights the flame under the aluminum foil. The puddle
crackles and pops, then starts to smoke --

                    SETH (cont'd)
              Go... Go!

There's a rush of thick grey smoke. Caroline catches most of
it.

                    SETH (cont'd)
              Hold it.

She pulls it in deeper and holds... Suddenly her expression
changes... Her eyes lose their focus, her face slackens, an
almost sexual response. Seth is watching her intensely.

                    SETH (cont'd)
              See... Now, you see.

Caroline slumps back against the counter. Seth moves against
her, kissing her, running his hands over her breasts and
body. She stares over his shoulder, holding it as long as she
can.

Finally she exhales --

                    CAROLINE
              More.

The cloud of grey smoke from her lungs fills the room.

                                                    CUT TO:

36   INT. WHITE HOUSE OFFICE - DAY   36

The White House CHIEF OF STAFF meets with Robert Wakefield.
The Chief of Staff has the floor; he always has the floor.
This is a man you do not want to disappoint.

                    CHIEF OF STAFF
              Until you officially take over the office
              of National Drug Control Policy, under no
              circumstances should you speak to the
              press unprotected, without going through
              this office or having someone in the
              room. There are a lot of interests in
              this town and, right now, they're all
              scared of you. The reason they're scared
              of you...technically, you have veto power
              over their budgets. So think about that:
              FBI, CIA, DEA, CUSTOMS, TREASURY, ATF,
              DEFENSE, IRS, Radio Shack and the DMV,
              they're all gonna want to speak to you.
                    (MORE)

                                              (CONTINUED)

CHIEF OF STAFF (cont'd)
And that's the good news... You'll also
be meeting Senators and Congressman, each
with a specially prepared question. Their
question is designed for one thing: to
make them look smart. If you lecture
them, they won't think you respect them.
If you respond with utter humility, they
will. Remember, this is about your
respect for them, and the President's
respect for them. Speaking of which, as
soon as he gets back from Russia and
China, we'll get you in there for some
face-time, let the two of you catch up.
(beat)
It'd probably be a good idea for you to
meet your predecessor. I'll have Jeff
Sheridan take you over. Also, four weeks
from today you will give your first
official press conference. In it you will
outline the President's strategy for
winning the war on drugs.
(beat)
Okay, anything else?

ROBERT
I'll be sure to let you know.

37   INT. EXECUTIVE BUILDING, WASHINGTON, D.C. - DAY   37

Robert makes his way through a warren of hallways in the
endless corridors of the Old Executive Building alongside
JEFF SHERIDAN, 35, an enthusiastic government employee who
has found his place.

SHERIDAN
I just want to be clear about one thing.
I used to work for him, but now I work
for you. I'm not a partisan person, I'm
an issue person. In the next few weeks,
if you allow me, we'll get you well-
versed on an incredible array of issues.
The most important of which, in my
opinion, being Mexico. I know everybody
that you're gonna meet. I know what they
want and why. It's important that they
like you. It's not important that they
like me. That's why I can help protect
you.

ROBERT
Like you protected Landry?

                         SHERIDAN
              I see where you're going with that, but
              if I could just say something, which is
              basically that a guy like Landry is so
              autocratic he doesn't know how to let
              himself be helped; it's a point of pride
              to take every bullet, no matter who fired
              it, or whether it was even aimed at him,
              which personally I think is very self-
              defeating. Now, don't get me wrong, he's
              a man of enormous integrity, but there's
              a political component to this job that
              the General just didn't have any patience
              for.

38   INT. OFFICE OF NATIONAL DRUG CONTROL POLICY - DAY   38

      Robert and Sheridan enter the office of outgoing Drug Czar,
      GENERAL RALPH LANDRY, 60's, buzz-cut, professional soldier
      with a sense of humor.

      Landry is putting some personal items in a box.

                         GENERAL LANDRY
              Jeff, you want to excuse us for a minute?

      Sheridan nods and leaves.

                         GENERAL LANDRY (cont'd)
                    (bemused, off Sheridan's exit)
              Functionaries. Nice people, the *Schedule
              C's*. About twelve graduate degrees
              apiece, but it seems sometimes all they
              do is start rumors.

      Robert and Landry shake hands.

                         ROBERT
              You've done a fine job here, Sir. The
              Office of National Drug Control Policy is
              in better shape than when you found it.

      Landry tries to determine whether Robert believes this. He
      looks around the office as if the policy is hiding somewhere.

                         GENERAL LANDRY
              I'm not sure I made the slightest
              difference.
                    (wistful)
              I tried... I really did.

                                                        (CONTINUED)

                    ROBERT
          There are a lot of encouraging
          statistics. The work's just started, but
          I intend to see it through. You've got my
          word on that.

                    GENERAL LANDRY
          You're here for two years, three maximum.
          What'd they promise you? Court
          appointment? What? District? Appeals?
                    (checks Robert's reaction)
          Not Supreme... Supreme?

                    ROBERT
          I've come in to do a tough job and that's
          what I'm going to focus on.

General Landry SIGHS.

                    GENERAL LANDRY
          When Kruschev was forced out, he sat down
          and wrote two letters and handed them to
          his successor. He said *When you get into
          a situation you can't get out of, open
          the first letter and you'll be saved. And
          when you get into another situation you
          can't get out of, open the second.* Soon
          enough this guy found himself in a tight
          place. So he opened the first letter. It
          said, *Blame everything on me.* So he
          blamed the old guy and it worked like a
          charm.
                    (beat)
          He got into another situation he couldn't
          get out of, so he opened the second
          letter, which read, *Sit down and write
          two letters.*

They stare at each other a beat. Then Landry smiles.

                                                    CUT TO:

39   EXT. MANOLO'S STREET, MEXICO - DAY   39

     A cinderblock house. Kids and dogs in the street. A face we
     recognize as Manolo's peers out of a curtain into the street.

40   INT. MANOLO'S KITCHEN - DAY   40

     The ceiling is stained, the floor sags. A cheap radio plays.
     Manolo is at the door. Javi sits at a dinette table.

                                                    (CONTINUED)

40   CONTINUED: 40

He talks to Manolo but watches Manolo's wife, ANNA, 20's, a
nice-looking, ostensibly demure young woman, as she moves
around the kitchen.

                    JAVIER
          Relax. If they were going to kill us they
          would have done it in the desert.

                    MANOLO
          They wouldn't do it in front of all those
          people. They'd send someone later, when
          we're alone.

Manolo tenses, and throws open the window.

                    MANOLO (V.O.) (CONT'D)
               (yelling out the window)
          Away from the car. Now!

MANOLO'S POV out the window as KIDS play in the car, sitting
behind the wheel.

                    JAVIER
          Even if that were true, they're not going
          to come to your house where you're
          waiting for them.

                    ANNA
          He's right. They'll do it when you're
          walking somewhere, make it look like
          street crime.

                    MANOLO
          Shut your fucking mouth. Nobody's talking
          to you.

Anna sets a cup of coffee in front of Javi and stares at him.

AA41 INT. POLICE SEDAN - DAY   AA41

Javi and Manolo cruise through the streets of Tijuana.

                    JAVIER
          If you want her to stay out of it, then
          stop telling her everything. You should
          learn how to keep a secret.

                    MANOLO
          She's nosy. She hears me on the
          telephone.

                    JAVIER
          Anyway, I don't think we'll ever see them
          again. Everything's back to normal.

A41 EXT. TIJUANA STREET - DAY   A41

Tourist hell. A cacophony of street venders, panhandlers, and
vehicular traffic. Javier and Manolo are speaking with a
flustered young American TOURIST COUPLE.

                         TOURIST WOMAN
               You're a police officer. Aren't you going
               to take a report or something? Don't you
               want to know what kind of car it is?

                         TOURIST MAN
               It's a Brown Ford Explorer --

                         TOURIST WOMAN
               It was right here. It's been stolen. I
               want to file a report.

                         MANOLO
               Please. Filing a report will not help you
               find your car.

                         JAVIER
               The police won't find your car.

                         TOURIST WOMAN
               But you're the police.

Javier pulls out a note pad and scribbles a number.

                         JAVIER
               Call this man, he'll find your car for
               you.

                         TOURIST MAN
               I don't get it --

                         TOURIST WOMAN
               How will this guy know who has our car?

                         JAVIER
               The police will tell him.

There's a beat of confusion.

                         TOURIST MAN
               Why will they tell him but they won't
               tell us?

                         TOURIST WOMAN
                    (getting it)
               Because we pay him, stupid.
                    (to Javier)
                    (MORE)

                                              (CONTINUED)

A41   CONTINUED: A41

                          TOURIST WOMAN (cont'd)
                    Right? And he pays the police. And then
                    our car appears.

                          JAVIER
                    Yes. Better than filling out forms,
                    right?

The man reaches in his wallet and offers Javier a twenty.
Javi waves him off.

Javier and Manolo walk back to their squad car when two
SUV's come to a stop in front of them.

Javier and Manolo exchange a look. The doors SLAM and
FOOTSTEPS approach.

                          OFFICER (O.S.)
                    Javier Rodriguez.

                                                          CUT TO:

41   EXT LA JOLLA GOLF AND TENNIS CLUB - DAY   41

A ladies luncheon in the Nancy Reagan Dining Room overlooking
a putting green. The bejewelled WIVES of successful men
yammer at one another around tables with rich flower
centerpieces.

SUPERTITLE: LA JOLLA, CALIFORNIA, JUST OUTSIDE SAN DIEGO

One wife, HELENA AYALA, 32, ex-model, with a sweetness and
intelligence that almost contradicts her beauty, stares out
the window at a small BOY, 5, using a putter as tall as he
is. Helena is six months pregnant and radiant.

A waiter brings Helena's starter course. Her friends, NAN
DOBBS, early 40's, post Junior League, a little tipsy, STEWIE
and ALEX, same League, watch her --

                          NAN
                    Duck salad?

                          HELENA
                    Mmm.

Nan can't believe it.

                          NAN
                    Helena, you never order duck salad.

                          HELENA
                    Well, that's true. I don't.
                         (re: her belly)
                    I think someone else is asking for it.

                                                      (CONTINUED)

> NAN
> Well, he's got good taste. Isn't it the most wonderful thing you ever tasted? I mean ever.

> HELENA
> It's delicious --

> STEWIE
> They're the most marvelous little creatures. Canard. They fly, swim, walk. And so cute with their babies marching along behind.

> NAN
> Looking for a nice sauce ala orange.

Everyone laughs. Helena is by far the youngest in her crowd.

> ALEX
> It's a very fatty bird. All that winter insulation. Just like me.

> NAN
> You mean all breast, just like you.

> ALEX
> You're bad --

> NAN
> (singsong)
> Jealous, that's all --

> HELENA
> I've heard... I can't remember where... That it's full of that good kind of fat, the kind you're supposed to eat --

> STEWIE
> Unsaturated fat --

> TWO WOMEN IN UNISON
> Polyunsaturated.

> HELENA
> And now there's good cholesterol and bad cholesterol. Everything they tell you completely changes every other week. I don't know why they think we should listen at all.

(CONTINUED)

41   CONTINUED: (2)   41

                         NAN
                What I know is ducks, as cute as they
                are, were designed by God to be eaten.

       Nan reaches for a taste and the other women lean forward
       also, a sea of inanity swirling around Helena's salad.

42   EXT. COUNTRY CLUB PARKING LOT - DAY   42

       Helena buckles her little boy, DAVID, 5, into the front seat
       of her Mercedes. He won't let go of his putter.

                         HELENA
                I'll put this in the back.

                         DAVID
                No --

                         HELENA
                All the professionals keep them in the
                trunk.

                         DAVID
                Not Tiger Woods.

                         HELENA
                Especially Tiger Woods.
                     (sharing a secret)
                ... Actually, he keeps his on the back
                seat.

       She pulls the putter away from the reluctant boy and sets it
       on the back seat.

43   EXT. HOTEL - DAY   43

       A modern high-rise on the waterfront playground of San Diego.

       Helena passes the hotel in her car.

44   INT. HOTEL ROOM - DAY   44

       A standard room looking out at the water which is dotted with
       sailboats and cruise ships. The bed is covered with hi-tech
       surveillance equipment.

       The equipment salesman, LONNIE, 40's, who makes a fetish of
       gadgetry, explains the finer points of operation to FRANCISCO
       "FRANKIE" FLORES, 30's, sallow, watery-eyed, in expensive
       clothes.

                                                  (CONTINUED)

                              LONNIE
               Gates, Myrhvold, Bezos. I sell to all
               those guys. Why? Because the technology
               to intrude has reached the masses. Your
               competitor, your ex-spouse, adversaries,
               stalkers, they're at the local
               electronics store right now, and they're
               gonna be intruding on you not only
               through your telephone, but your fax,
               cell phone, pager, cable TV, Musak,
               windows, walls, air conditioning
               ventilation, modem, and internet
               connection.

He walks over to the bed and the sexy equipment --

                              LONNIE (cont'd)
               Nobody has these babies, no way, not the
               shiznit.

Frederico picks up a piece of equipment.

                              FRANCISCO
               I want to intercept cell phone calls,
               digital and analog. And locate the source
               of the call. I need databasing
               capability, to cross-reference calls and
               numbers.

Lonnie lovingly picks up a laptop computer with a sleek
device attached to it --

                              LONNIE
               Your Cellular Secretary, friend across
               all the digital wireless spread spectrum.
                    (beat)
               So, Francisco, what do you do? You a PI?
               Private security?

Francisco looks at Lonnie coldly.

                              FRANCISCO
               Assassin.

                              LONNIE
                    (not missing a beat)
               Assassin, okay. Let's get you started in
               surveillance.

                                                        CUT TO:

45   EXT. GEORGETOWN BROWNSTONE - NIGHT   45

      The house takes up most of one of the nicest blocks. PEOPLE
      enter and party VOICES drift out.

      SUPERTITLE: GEORGETOWN, WASHINGTON, D.C.

46   INT. GEORGETOWN BROWNSTONE - NIGHT   46

      A power cocktail party in full swing. This is where most of
      the business in Washington gets done.

      Robert, scotch in hand, listens to a smug PHARMACEUTICAL
      LOBBYIST explain the world.

                         PHARMACEUTICAL LOBBYIST
                  We in the legal drug business, and I mean
                  Merck, Pfizer, the rest of my very
                  powerful clients, realize this isn't a
                  war with a traditional winner and loser,
                  but an organism at war with itself, whose
                  weapons of mass destruction happen to be
                  intoxicants. And if you want a body count
                  look no further than alcohol which racks
                  up 80,000 kills a year. Cocaine manages a
                  measly 2,000. Same for Heroin. But, the
                  big daddy is Big Tobacco which kills
                  380,000 each year, which, by the way, is
                  more people than have been killed by all
                  the illegal drugs in the last century.

                         ROBERT
                     (faking it)
                  That's very interesting.

      The lobbyist smiles. Robert sips his drink.

47   ANOTHER ANGLE ON ROBERT   47

      in another room. Listening to STAN, overweight advocate for
      the United States Council of Chambers of Commerce.

                         STAN
                  It's time, Robert, to choke some honesty
                  out of these rural legislators; get 'em
                  to fess up that it's pretty much Prisons
                  or Casinos in terms of their choices for
                  economic growth.

48   ANOTHER ANGLE ON ROBERT   48

      listening to ETHAN, earnest advocate of harm reduction.

                                                   (CONTINUED)

> ETHAN
> What's the difference between Prozac and
> Ecstacy, you ask? One's a mattress and
> the other's a trampoline. Molecules
> don't have morality. Really, think about
> it: some molecule changes the way a
> serotonin re-uptake inhibitor works, it's
> not suddenly a bad molecule; it's just a
> molecule. My theory: America has a real
> fear of short, intense experiences.

Robert turns away --

> ROBERT
> (under his breath)
> Like you.

49   ANOTHER ROOM   49

Robert at the bar getting another scotch. A secretive man,
TIM, 40's, nerdy, sidles up beside him and whispers furtively
in his ear.

> TIM
> (whispering)
> Chemicals? Some say problem, others say
> solution. Imagine a cloud that when it
> rains prohibits the growth of poppies or
> takes the THC out of marijuana. Imagine a
> pill that eliminates any psychological
> craving, from Dilaudid to Dove Bars. Law
> enforcement hasn't let science sit on the
> sidelines. Addiction is no more relevant
> than polio or the Black Plague.

Tim slips away into the crowd. Robert moves away from the
bar.

50   ANOTHER ROOM   50

An argument is breaking out between an ECONOMIST and an
UNDERSECRETARY OF DEFENSE with Robert as the audience.

> ECONOMIST
> (to the undersecretary)
> You're not battling traffickers or
> dealers, but a market, and the market
> contains a paradox: if you arrest
> traffickers, you raise prices, and you
> also raise profits, which brings more
> traffickers into the business.

                          UNDERSECRETARY
                    (to the Economist)
               Back in the real world, we're talking
               about Mexico and not John Maynard Keynes.
               We will spend 18 billion dollars this
               year on this "war," and the question on
               the table every year is do we certify
               Mexico as an ally or not?

Another man, RUSH PHILLIPS, a middle-aged powerbroker,
overhears, then joins and Robert is encircled.

                          RUSH PHILLIPS
               You want to make a difference, hit the
               users. You don't jeopardize our financial
               markets by some hypocritical stance on
               drug consumption. We're snorting it, why
               penalize Mexico for supplying it?

                          UNDERSECRETARY
               Mexico, don't talk to me about Mexico --

                          ECONOMIST
               It's the stick of law enforcement that
               creates the carrot of huge profits...
               That's economic truth --

                          RUSH PHILLIPS
               Addicts don't vote; they don't have PACs;
               they don't spend soft money, that's
               political truth --

                          UNDERSECRETARY
               We're locking them up and consumption is
               falling --

                          ECONOMIST
               The price of coke and heroin has dropped
               and purity has increased. All this law
               enforcement has achieved is kids can get
               better stuff, cheaper. In economic terms,
               you can forget it; this is not a winnable
               war.

                          RUSH PHILLIPS
               Christ, you want to decertify somebody,
               take Pakistan or Columbia. We don't need
               them for anything.

                                                 (CONTINUED)

                        ECONOMIST
        If you manage to seize an inconceivable
        50 percent of all drugs coming into this
        country, you'll still raise the price of
        coke and heroin less than 3 percent which
        won't affect drug use at all.

                        RUSH PHILLIPS
        Why are we calling this a war at all? You
        don't declare war on your own people.
        Addiction is a little worm that gnaws a
        house apart from the inside.

MICHAEL ADLER, about Robert's age, and as successful, but in
a different way, approaches, catching Robert's eye through
the arguing demagogues.

                        UNDERSECRETARY
        We need Mexico for these reasons: number
        one -- Defense; two -- Trade; three --
        Tourism; then, way on down the line,
        comes Drugs. The President knows this.
        Why's he holding everybody's feet to the
        fire?

                        MICHAEL
                (solemn)
        Mr. Wakefield, there's a situation that
        needs your attention right away.

Robert looks at Michael, squints, looks closer, then follows.

                        RUSH PHILLIPS
                (oblivious)
        One in sixteen Americans is of Mexican
        descent. Mexico our third largest trading
        partner...

51   ANGLE ON ROBERT AND MICHAEL   51

on the back porch.

                        ROBERT
        You're looking pretty good for an old
        guy.

                        MICHAEL
        My work keeps me young.

                        ROBERT
        Which part, getting terrorists loose on
        bail or freeing convicted murderers on
        technicalities?

                                            (CONTINUED)

                        MICHAEL
            The worst serial killer in history - who?
            Gacy - right? Killed forty two people.
            Our government killed fifty thousand in
            Vietnam and lied about it every day.

                        ROBERT
            Michael, you represent drug dealers, not
            civil libertarians.

                        MICHAEL
            We kidnapped Noriega out of Panama. Is
            that covered in your Constitution?
            Because it isn't in mine.

                        ROBERT
            Noriega is a criminal.

                        MICHAEL
            Noriega was head of a sovereign nation
            who made the mistake of doing business
            with the U.S. Government. So, no, I don't
            have a problem waking up every day and
            fighting our government, fighting people
            like you, trying to keep this system a
            little bit honest.

                        ROBERT
                (amused)
            Last I read your clients were chopping
            people up with chainsaws and delivering
            illegal narcotics into this country.

                        MICHAEL
            I hope when you were on the bench, Judge
            Wakefield, you didn't handle the
            presumption of innocence in the same
            fashion.

                        ROBERT
            If I ever return to the bench, Counselor
            Adler, I hope I have the pleasure of
            hearing your arguments.

                                                        CUT TO:

52   INT. HOSPITAL EMERGENCY ROOM, SAN DIEGO - DAY   52

      Eduardo Ruiz lies in a hospital bed, handcuffed to the
      railing. His bandaged foot is held aloft by a sling and a
      tube drains the wound. He is tugging on the handcuffs as
      Castro and Gordon enter the room.

                                                    (CONTINUED)

                              GORDON
                    You planning on going somewhere, Eduardo?
                    You don't like it here? This is the best
                    situation you're going to have for a
                    long, long time.

                              RUIZ
                    I am a legitimate businessman. Fishing
                    boats. Tuna. Check it out. Tax records,
                    everything --

                              GORDON
                    Listen you motherfucker, you tried to
                    kill me with a fucking cannon.

                              RUIZ
                    You can't visit me here. I want my
                    lawyer.

                              GORDON
                    The amount of coke we got on you means
                    capital punishment in some states.

                              CASTRO
                    Move 'em to Texas, fry 'em up.

                              GORDON
                    We got you on tape making the deal. We
                    got you bragging about the quality. We
                    got you bragging about your business. We
                    got you.

        A NURSE appears in the doorway. Gordon goes to the door and
        shuts it in her face.

                              GORDON (cont'd)
                    One chance here, Eduardo. Make us believe
                    you got a boss. No boss, it's all on you.

                              RUIZ
                    It's a death sentence. I'll never make it
                    to the trial.

                              GORDON
                    We can protect you.

        Ruiz looks at them in disbelief.

                              CASTRO
                    Who do you work for?

                              RUIZ
                    This is coercion.

                                                  (CONTINUED)

52   CONTINUED: (2)   52

                              GORDON
                    That's a big word for a fisherman.

                              CASTRO
                    Who do you work for?

          Gordon and Ruiz stare at each other.

                              RUIZ
                    I know another word... Immunity.

                                                          CUT TO:

53   EXT. AYALA HOME - LA JOLLA - DAY   53

          A starter castle high in the hills near Mount Soledad, an
          exclusive neighborhood with views of the ocean. Joggers jog
          to the SOUNDS of tennis and Jacuzzis gurgling, and lawn care
          equipment operated by Mexicans.

          Behind the Ayala gate we see David playing with his golf club
          on the lush lawn.

          Workers set-up the party under the direction of a
          professional party planner.

          A BMW 740il with tinted windows pulls into the driveway.

                              DAVID
                    Daddy!

          The window lowers and we see CARL AYALA, 40's, handsome,
          charismatic, second generation American, in expensive,
          conservative clothes, covering his cell phone as he greets
          his kids.

                              CARL
                    Hello. Hello.

          He goes back to his phone call, pulling around to the garage.
          David goes back to his game.

54   INT. AYALA DINING ROOM - DAY   54

          There are MAIDS in the house and a COOK in the kitchen. The
          large rooms are filled with fine art.

          Helena Ayala sits at the dining room table with plans, bills
          and receipts spread before her. Carl enters and paces around
          the room, continuing his cell phone conversation.

                                                          (CONTINUED)

                         CARL
                     (into phone)
                 I'm sorry, Jonas. I don't care if that is
                 the price you have gotten in other
                 countries.

Helena watches her husband pace as he talks. He can't help
it, but a portion of this call is theatrical, for an
audience's benefit, which in this instance happens to be his
wife. Helena's expression of annoyance resets itself into
love.

                         CARL (cont'd)
                 This is America, a different country. I
                 am Carl, a different man. So you see,
                 everything about our situation is
                 different and I believe the pricing will
                 be different, too.
                     (beat, listens)
                 You're a reasonable man... So take the
                 weekend to think about it.

Carl clicks off the phone, turns to Helena.

                         CARL (cont'd)
                 Every day with this guy is like starting
                 all over again.

Carl winds down and finally becomes present in the room with
his wife. He looks at her. She looks back.

                         CARL (cont'd)
                 Hi.

                         HELENA
                 Hi.

                         CARL
                 What's up?

                         HELENA
                 Just watching you.

                         CARL
                 I got that. How was your day?

She pushes the topiary away from her. Suddenly, she seems
tired. Carl comes over and puts his hand on her pregnant
belly.

                         CARL (cont'd)
                 You all right?

                                                  (CONTINUED)

54   CONTINUED: (2)   54

                         HELENA
                  I keep feeling like I'm forgetting
                  something.

Her husband watches her, then wraps his arms around her.

55   EXT. AYALA HOME - DAY   55

Carl and Helena step out on the front porch of their home and
watch David play with his golf putter.

OUTSIDE THEIR GATE

An unmarked police car rolls up and stops behind the wall.
Another arrives and another and another. OFFICERS in DEA
jackets exit the cars.

There is MURMURING, then SILENCE.

Helena slowly turns to look at her husband. He doesn't look
at her.

                         HELENA
                  David, come inside --

Suddenly, POLICE and DEA enter the front yard. Gordon and
Castro enter the yard and move quickly up the drive to Carl.

                         CARL
                  What is this? What is going on?

                         GORDON
                  Mr. Ayala?

                         CARL
                  That's right.

                         GORDON
                  You're under arrest for violation of
                  Federal Narcotics laws.

Gordon and Castro spin him, cuff him, and without emotion
begin pulling him from his yard. David is trying to get to
his father. In a kind of shock. Helena trails after him.

Castro drags Carl into the street toward the open door of the
cruiser. He pushes him down into the backseat.

                         GORDON (CONT'D)
                  We have a warrant to search your home,
                  Mrs. Ayala.

                                                        (CONTINUED)

Gordon hits the side of the cruiser and it pulls away. Carl
looks at his wife through the window.

Gordon and Castro head up the driveway toward her house.
Helena is left standing in the street. NEIGHBORS, who have
appeared in front yards and at the ends of driveways, stare
at her with suspicion. David approaches and holds onto her
leg.

                                                        CUT TO:

56   OMITTED   56

A57   INT. SALAZAR'S HEADQUARTERS - ANTEROOM - DAY   A57

Javi and Manolo wait in Salazar's anteroom. A ceiling fan
swirls the air. After a moment the door opens and an AIDE
motions to them. They stand.

                        AIDE
                  (to Manolo)
            Not you. You.

Javi goes into the room.

57   INT. SALAZAR'S OFFICE - DAY   57

The office is Spartan and military. Salazar and Javi sit
facing each other. Salazar looks at a piece of paper.

                        SALAZAR
            Javier Rodriguez. Twenty-nine years-old.
            Graduated from Montessori school. Five
            years as a beat cop in TJ. Three years
            with the State Police. Parents died four
            years ago in their apartment from carbon
            monoxide poisoning because they could not
            afford to fix their gas heater. Your
            sister works in a Maquiladora in Juarez,
            making designer blue-jeans. On the police
            force three years, you currently make 316
            dollars a month.

Salazar crumples the piece of paper and tosses it in the
trash.

                        SALAZAR (cont'd)
            That's your past. I want to talk about
            your future. Would you be willing to do
            something for me?

                        JAVIER
            If I can.

                                                   (CONTINUED)

57   CONTINUED: 57

                        SALAZAR
              I'm trying to bust the Tijuana Cartel.

                        JAVIER
              What is it you want me to do?

                        SALAZAR
              A small thing. Nothing really.

         Javier thinks about this.

                        JAVIER
              Does this offer include my partner?

                        SALAZAR
              Only if he can be trusted.

                        JAVIER
              He'll do what I say.

         Salazar slides a folder across the desk. Javier opens it and
         sees a black and white surveillance photo of the informant.

                        SALAZAR
              His name is Francisco Flores. He is a
              killer and gun smuggler for the Tijuana
              cartel. I need to speak with him. I need
              you to find him and bring him to me so
              that I can speak with him.

A58   INT. POLICE SEDAN - DAY   A58

         Manolo faces Javier.

                        MANOLO
              This is fucking crazy. Instead of killing
              us, he sends us on a suicide mission. Do
              you know who Frankie Flowers is? He's a
              psycho-cokehead-hitman. A faggot. He's
              killed fucking who knows how many people.
              You'd need half the force to get close to
              him. And you can't get their help because
              he lives in fucking San Diego.

                        JAVIER
              Then I guess I'm going by myself.

                                                          CUT TO:

58   INT. AIRPLANE - DAY   58

         Robert Wakefield sits in business class. He twists the cap
         off a mini-bottle of bourbon and pours it over a cup of ice.

                                                    (CONTINUED)

58   CONTINUED: 58

        He empties a second bottle into the cup, then swirls it
        around on the ice. He takes a sip.

59   INT. AIRPORT GATE - DAY   59

        Robert exits with his briefcase and hanging bag, two SECURITY
        MEN trailing him. He sees Barbara and Caroline, his wife and
        daughter, waiting by the their station wagon. They wave.

60   INT. CAR - DAY   60

        On the way home from the airport. Caroline drives carefully
        with Barbara in the front seat and Robert in back.

                              ROBERT
                    What's it like?
                         (thinks)
                    Imagine you're being accosted by a swarm
                    of beggars in the heart of Calcutta,
                    except the beggars are wearing $1500
                    suits and they don't say "please" or
                    "thank you".

                              CAROLINE
                    What about legalizing everything? Has
                    anybody talked about that?

                              ROBERT
                    Fine -- legalization. Okay, forgetting
                    all of our international trade
                    agreements, legalize everything today.
                    The Government inserts itself into all
                    drug transactions. The U.S. becomes a
                    giant pharmacy. Our borders are mobbed,
                    lines of people from here to Europe
                    wanting to smoke, snort and shoot
                    themselves into oblivion.

                              BARBARA
                         (lightly)
                    Like a Grateful Dead Concert.

                              ROBERT
                    Drugs begin pouring out of America into
                    every other country in the world. Canada
                    is completely overwhelmed.

                              CAROLINE
                    What if every country legalized at the
                    same time?

                              ROBERT
                         (smiles)
                    Somehow, I don't see that happening.

61   INT. WAKEFIELD DINING ROOM - EVENING   61

From the hallway we see Robert and Barbara and Caroline
having dinner. A family tableau. We hear Barbara talking, the
murmur of the days events.

In the room, Barbara continues her dinner table thoughts.
Robert has a good deal of reading material stacked on the
table.

> BARBARA
> So you know we put the case before the
> arbitration panel, none of whom had any
> expertise. Superfund is just one of those
> words. People stop paying attention.

> ROBERT
> That's frustrating.

> BARBARA
> It's so frustrating.

There is wine on the table and Caroline is allowed a glass.
Her parents watch her take a responsible sip.

> CAROLINE
> (to Robert)
> Did you meet the President?

> BARBARA
> Honey, your father knows the President.

> ROBERT
> As it happens, the President of the
> United States, my new boss, the leader of
> the free world, has me pencilled in for
> some "face time".

> CAROLINE
> Will we get invited to the White House?

> ROBERT
> I don't know.

> CAROLINE
> How long's the job?

> ROBERT
> It's a presidential appointment so...
> until I quit or get fired.

> BARBARA
> Czar for life, just like a real czar.

                        (CONTINUED)

> CAROLINE
> That makes mom the Czarina. I'm a
> Czarette. Like Anastasia.

Caroline thinks about this.

> CAROLINE (CONT'D)
> None of my friends can fucking believe my
> dad is the actual Drug Czar.

> BARBARA
> Caroline --

> CAROLINE
> Sorry, but I mean, come on.

Robert doesn't know if she's putting him down.

> CAROLINE (CONT'D)
> It's great, daddy. It's just amazing,
> that's all.

They all look at each other. Caroline sips her wine.

                                                      CUT TO:

62   INT. SAN DIEGO JAIL - DAY   62

In the intake area of a busy San Diego precinct, Helena sits
on a bench and regroups. Detectives move past her. Handcuffed
criminals are separated, bagged and tagged.

A beautifully dressed man, ARNIE METZGER, 30's, super-lawyer,
knows everyone from the top of the system to the bottom,
slick but likable, smart and ruthless, too, separates himself
from a DETECTIVE he's gladhanding and approaches Helena.

> METZGER
> Helena, I'm so sorry --

> HELENA
> Arnie, thank God.

Metzger sits, giving her a hug.

> HELENA (cont'd)
> Can you please tell me what on earth is
> going on?

Arnie looks at her as if to say, "do you really not know?"
Then, he speaks quietly with his hand in front of his mouth.

                                                  (CONTINUED)

>   METZGER
>   I understand. You're upset. You want to
>   know what's going on. That's good.

>   HELENA
>   Why are you talking like that?

>   METZGER
>   Listen to me carefully. First of all,
>   Carl isn't here. DEA's got him and
>   they'll hang on to him until arraignment,
>   which will probably be tomorrow. So here
>   you're wasting your time. Are you with
>   me?

He checks to see if this is registering.

>   METZGER (cont'd)
>   Good. From now on I want you to expect
>   that every word you utter will be tape-
>   recorded, that the movement of your lips
>   is being read. Got it?

>   HELENA
>   Arnie, this is crazy.

He makes eye contact with her.

>   METZGER
>   Got it?
>   (she slowly nods)
>   Good. Do not discuss anything over the
>   telephone. Do not talk to the neighbors.
>   Stay out of your yard.

>   HELENA
>   What is he being charged with?

>   METZGER
>   I don't know, but under no circumstances
>   would I talk about it here. I want you to
>   go home and relax the best you can.
>   Continue your life as if nothing has
>   happened. That is very important.

>   HELENA
>   Arnie, I feel like Alice stepping through
>   the looking glass.

>   METZGER
>   That's a very apt analogy, Helena. Now,
>   go home and be with your children.

63   EXT. BUILDING PARKING LOT - DAY   63

        Helena exits. Her expression is set as she drives. She turns
        a corner in the shopping district, passing

        JAVIER AND MANOLO

        who are walking down the street. Tourists, drunk Marines and
        the homeless piss away another day.

        We follow them into a bar with blackened windows and a
        discrete sign.

64   INT. BAR - DAY   64

        This is a place where men come to meet men. And it's already
        lively even at this early hour. Javier and Manolo find a seat
        and wait.

        LATER

        Javi is working on his second beer when he seems to recognize
        somebody.

        ACROSS THE ROOM

        Francisco "Frankie" Flowers has entered the bar. Javi watches
        him circulate through the room then settle at the bar. Javier
        finishes his beer, rises, and takes the empty seat next to
        Francisco. Manolo watches.

        Very quickly Javi strikes up a conversation. We don't hear
        what they're saying but it doesn't matter because Francisco
        clearly likes Javi.

        Off Francisco's anticipatory smile --

65   OMITTED   65

66   OMITTED   66

67   EXT. MILITARY BASE - MEXICO - DAY   67

        The back of a blue van opens and a blindfolded Francisco
        falls onto the ground.

        Surrounding him are Javi and Salazar, who watch as two of
        Salazar's MEN drag Francisco away toward an abandoned mission-
        style building.

                                                (CONTINUED)

67   CONTINUED: 67

                    SALAZAR
                (clearly pleased with Javi)
            I'm curious how you did this with such
            economy.

                    JAVIER
            Everybody has a weakness.

                                            CUT TO:

68 EXT. SOMEBODY'S PARENTS' MANSION, CINCINNATI - NIGHT   68

With its old-growth trees and manipulated shrubbery, the
large house is shrouded in the mystery of well-heeled
suburbia. It is very late.

69 INT. SOMEBODY'S PARENTS' MANSION - NIGHT   69

Somebody's parents are out of town and the house feels empty.
Big empty rooms with expensive furniture nobody sits on.
Faint MUSIC echoes through the house.

70 INT. KITCHEN - NIGHT   70

High ceilings of a 1930's kitchen. Vodka bottles and
cranberry juice and limes are spilled across a counter. ON
THE RHODES AGAIN by Morcheeba plays from a jam-box on a
counter.

Maybe ten TEENAGERS are partying hard in this kitchen. It's
weird and disassociated, people wandering in and out, playing
with kitchen utensils, heavily fucked up.

There are drugs on a mirror on the eat-in table. Caroline and
Seth and two friends sit around this table. VANESSA, 16,
almost pretty, is hitting a freebase pipe and holds the hit.
FUCKED-UP BOWMAN, 17, super-preppy with a wan, Baby Huey
face, takes a slug of vodka.

They are jittery, sweaty, tweaked, fucked-up --

                    CAROLINE
            All I'm saying, what I'm saying, is it
            never seems like anybody ever says
            anything that matters to them, like we
            all look at each other and nod with
            responses we've been trained to make, not
            real responses, just social conventions,
            phony, fake smiles, surface bullshit... I
            mean, we're all smart and do we have any
            idea what each other are like, really
            like? Do I know what Seth's afraid of, or
            Vanessa, or fucked-up Bowman?

                                        (CONTINUED)

Everyone looks at Fucked-up Bowman who grinds his jaw
appreciatively --

> CAROLINE (cont'd)
> ... Probably, but do I ever say this
> stuff, just say, "hey, I'm uncomfortable
> in this crowd, I don't know what the fuck
> I'm doing, either? I know you're afraid
> and it's okay --"

Seth's words come quickly, they're riffing, totally in sync,
totally wired --

> SETH
> We act like we have all the answers and
> we're totally invincible like our parents
> seem and their parents before them and
> it's fucking bullshit --

Fucked-up Bowman takes another slug of vodka and almost
pukes.

> FUCKED-UP BOWMAN
> For instance --

> SETH
> For instance I know you jack-off thinking
> about Caroline even though you're
> supposedly "in love" with Vanessa.
> Whatever the fuck that means?
> (a digression)
> I mean, what is that convention, anyway?
> We're all these random collections of
> self-interest, and then we just decide
> that now we're two people walking along --

Caroline expels a hit of rock cocaine --

> CAROLINE
> And Vanessa doesn't think she's pretty so
> she does all these weird fucking diets
> which is totally about self-esteem. And
> she's beautiful.
> (beat)
> And that's not even fair. Because listen
> to me. I'm fucking lying right now. This
> is exactly what I'm talking about... I'm
> supposedly talking about you, making some
> big point about you, and it's really
> about me. So I should talk about me, not
> you, not even the universal "you..."
> (takes a beat)
> Okay.
> (MORE)

                                                        (CONTINUED)

> CAROLINE (cont'd)
> Okay, I'm worried I'm not really smart or
> that I'm not nearly as smart as people
> think I am, or that my parents'
> expectations have been way too high since
> I was five, I mean who knows they're
> going to Harvard when they're five, not
> that I'm blaming them for anything
> because everything's great, and I may not
> even get in, but we all feel this shit
> and we never acknowledge it and if we
> can't acknowledge it to the people we
> care the most about then who will we ever
> say it too and what kind of life will
> that be?

They all look at each other with love. This is an adventure
and they're having a connection --

> FUCKED-UP BOWMAN
> I jack-off thinking about Seth. Everybody
> I know does.

Bowman does another huge hit of freebase.

> CAROLINE
>   (disgusted)
> Ach, that's what I'm talking about.
> Sarcasm. Always fucking sarcasm. You're
> afraid and you think if you admit it
> people will think you're weak or won't
> like you --

> SETH
> We live our lives by these unspoken rules
> that are handed to us.

They all look at each other, vibrating with the moment --

> VANESSA
> Let's be different --

> FUCKED-UP BOWMAN
> I can't feel my hands.

Bowman looks around, squinting, confused. He's chalk white.

> FUCKED-UP BOWMAN (cont'd)
> I'm serious --

Suddenly, he clutches his chest and begins to twitch. Puke
and foam come from his mouth. He seizes and falls from the
chair. Vanessa SCREAMS.

(CONTINUED)

> Seth and Caroline push the table aside to get a better look.
> Other people in the kitchen slowly take notice.

>> VANESSA
>> He's blue. He isn't breathing --

>> CAROLINE
>> Is he breathing?

> Bowman's eyes have rolled back in his head.

>> SETH
>> What do we do? Okay. Fucked-up Bowman's
>> turning blue. Doctor. We need a doctor.

>> VANESSA
>> Your dad's a doctor. Call him --

>> SETH
>> He's a research doctor. You're dad's a
>> doctor, too --

>> VANESSA
>> What kind of research?

>> SETH
>> Mapping the fucking pig genome. We'll
>> call your dad, he's a neurosurgeon --

>> VANESSA
>> It's three a.m. I'm not supposed to be
>> here. I snuck out --

>> CAROLINE
>> Are you kidding... I'm staying with you --

>> SETH
>> He's gonna fucking die right here on the
>> kitchen floor --

>> ANOTHER KID
>> He can't. My parents are in Barbados --

71   OMITTED   7

72   EXT. SUBURBAN HOSPITAL EMERGENCY ENTRANCE - NIGHT   7

> The Taurus wagon races up to the emergency room of Suburban
> Hospital. The back door opens and Bowman tumbles out onto the
> wheelchair ramp under the fluorescent lights.

> The car screeches around the circle --

(CONTINUED)

72   CONTINUED: 72

ACROSS THE PARKING LOT

TWO OFFICERS in a police car see the body tumble out of the car.

The cop car wheels around and cuts off the egress of the Taurus wagon --

73   INT. FORD TAURUS WAGON - NIGHT   73

Seth is behind the wheel. Caroline and Vanessa are in the back. They stare out at the cops getting out of the cruiser.

> SETH
> Nobody has anything on them, right?

                                              CUT TO:

74   OMITTED   74

75   INT. TORTURE ROOM - BARRACKS - DAY   75

Francisco is strapped naked into a chair. Duct tape covers his mouth. His face is bruised and swollen. A cruel TORTURER talks to him calmly while dumping chili powder into a container of soda water.

> TORTURER
> We know Tijuana Cartel gunmen killed our
> chief of intelligence, Francisco. We know
> you killed police commanders in Tijuana
> and Mexico City. Why do you resist?

He approaches Francisco and begins shaking up the soda water. He rips the tape off his mouth.

> FRANCISCO
> My father is rich. He'll pay you.

> TORTURER
> Not the correct answer, my friend.

The torturer puts another strip of duct tape across Francisco's mouth.

> TORTURER (cont'd)
> We know that you went after the neighbor
> of General Salazar, a simple alfalfa
> farmer. His grand-daughter was shot. This
> is stupid behavior, Francisco.

                                         (CONTINUED)

Francisco starts to squirm and whimper. The torturer closes
one of Francisco's nostrils and sprays the pepper-laced water
into the other nostril.

It's like a bomb went off in Francisco's brain. He SCREAMS
and passes out. Blood and mucous oozes out of his nose.

76   INT. BARRACKS - MEXICAN MILITARY BASE - DAY   76

Javier stands guard outside a door, listening to the
strangulated SCREAMS of Francisco. He's sickened.

ACROSS THE COURTYARD

Manolo ignores Francisco's CRIES, while shooting the shit
with several of Salazar's MEN, who laugh appreciatively at
something he's said.

                                                    CUT TO:

77   EXT. AYALA HOME, SAN DIEGO - NIGHT   77

Valet parkers in uniforms work the driveway. The party is
ablaze and there are lights in the trees. A Lester Lanin-like
band plays a STANDARD that drifts across the grounds.

78   EXT. AYALA HOME - NIGHT   78

A conservative monied crowd mingles. Helena is talking with a
GROUP of rich people who include her friends, Nan, Stewie and
Alex, from the country-club, and their HUSBANDS.

                         STEWIE
              This is fabulous, Helena. What a turnout.

                         HELENA
              Thank you so much, but I had a lot of
              help.

Helena circles away. As Helena leaves, the women speak their
minds --

                         NAN
              It's a turnout because it's a spectacle.
              Can you imagine?

                         ALEX
              I've met her husband, as nice as they
              come.

                                                    (CONTINUED)

>   STEWIE
>   It teaches me a valuable lesson...
>   (re: the nice house)
>   Apparently crime pays.

>   NAN
>   Silly, you knew that already.

ON THE STAGE

The band stops playing and steps aside as a man in a tuxedo
takes the microphone. Behind the band is a huge "A.L.A. -
Adult Literacy Advocates" Banner.

>   TUXEDO
>   Hello. Thank you. Thank you all. I have
>   the results of the silent auction...

                                                    CUT TO:

79   INT. JUVENILE DETENTION, CINCINNATI - HOLDING CELL - MORNING 79

Caroline Wakefield lies on a bench in a grey-walled holding
cell. She wears paper slippers and her belt has been removed.
Even youth can't disguise her hangover.

80   INT. SOCIAL WORKER OFFICE - MORNING   80

Caroline is perched on the edge of her chair. Across the desk
from her is a tired SOCIAL WORKER, 40's, who has been
assigned Caroline's case and is giving her the "exit"
interview.

>   SOCIAL WORKER
>   ... How old are you?

>   CAROLINE
>   Sixteen.

>   SOCIAL WORKER
>   Live with your parents?

>   CAROLINE
>   Yes.

>   SOCIAL WORKER
>   Parents still together?

>   CAROLINE
>   Yes.

>   SOCIAL WORKER
>   Do you work?

                                                    (CONTINUED)

                         CAROLINE
          I volunteer. I read to blind people. One
          day a week for two hours.

                         SOCIAL WORKER
          In school?

                         CAROLINE
          Cincinnati Country Day.

The Social worker looks up from her questionnaire and sees
Caroline for the first time.

                         SOCIAL WORKER
          Private?

                         CAROLINE
          Yeah.

                         SOCIAL WORKER
          How are your grades?

                         CAROLINE
          I'm third in my class.

                         SOCIAL WORKER
          What's that mean?

                         CAROLINE
          I get A's. All A's.

                         SOCIAL WORKER
          You do? What else you do?

                         CAROLINE
               (her college resume)
          I'm a National Merit Finalist. I'm on the
          Hi-Q team and the Math team. I'm in the
          Spanish Club. I'm a Thespian. I'm Vice-
          President of my class. I'm on the
          volleyball team.

The social worker pushes the forms she's filling out away
and looks again at Caroline --

                         SOCIAL WORKER
          You wanna tell me what you're doing here,
          Caroline?

81   INT. JUVENILE DETENTION - MORNING   81

A cold institutional lobby with hard plastic chairs and bad
lighting. Government workers move behind thick glass windows
with tiny mesh screens cut into them for talking.

Barbara Wakefield sits on one of the uncomfortable chairs.
She's alone and has been crying. There's the sound of heavily
locked doors OPENING and Caroline appears.

Barbara stands and wraps Caroline in her arms.

                    BARBARA
            Oh, honey. Are you all right?

Caroline begins to cry into her mother's chest.

82   EXT. JUVI JAIL - MORNING   82

It's an early morning as Barbara Wakefield escorts her
daughter from the bland government building.

                    CAROLINE
            Did you tell Dad?

                    BARBARA
            Not yet.

                    CAROLINE
            Are you going to?

                    BARBARA
            I don't know.

                    CAROLINE
            Is this bad for him?

                    BARBARA
            What do you think?

The streets are deserted. Their Saab wagon sits forlornly
under grey skies in an uncovered public parking lot.

CUT TO:

83   INT. DAVID'S ROOM - NIGHT   83

Helena slips into David's room and quietly watches him sleep.

84   INT. STUDY - LATER   84

Still wearing her evening gown, Helena collapses into a
chair, exhausted. A TAP at the door startles her.

                                        (CONTINUED)

84   CONTINUED: 84

It's Arnie Metzger, who goes to the bar and pours himself a
strong one. They sit opposite each other and neither speaks
for a while.

                    HELENA
                (quietly)
        I am on the board of my son's school. I
        had a fundraiser for A.L.V. in my front
        yard. I have a right to know if my
        husband is a legitimate businessman.

                    METZGER
        Of course he is. I've known him for
        twenty years and he doesn't jaywalk...

Helena is relieved, but she's not looking at Arnie and when
she does she sees him shaking his head in a very definitive,
"No."

Arnie stands and continues talking as he walks to the windows
and shuts the blinds one by one.

                    METZGER (cont'd)
        ... Carl is a very important member of
        this community and when we're through
        suing the police and the district
        attorney and the DEA, they'll have to
        rename the public parks for your husband.

The blinds are closed. Arnie crosses to Helena and talks very
softly in her ear. She's a beautiful woman and Arnie manages
to make this act seem both practical and inappropriate.

                    METZGER (cont'd)
                (whispering)
        Your husband is very good at his job...

Helena leans back and looks at Arnie. He whispers more --

                    METZGER (cont'd)
        Which is smuggling illegal drugs into
        this country.

85   EXT. AYALA HOME - NIGHT   85

Workers break down the party under the watchful eye of the
party planner. The neighborhood is quiet. There is a
telephone repair van parked up the street.

86   INT. VAN - NIGHT   86

Castro and Gordon have visual and audio equipment trained on
the Ayala home. They both wear headsets.

                                              (CONTINUED)

GORDON'S POV: the blinds covering Helena's study glowing
peacefully.

                        CASTRO
            They're whispering. I can't hear them,
            but I know it. I smell conspiracy. I feel
            the lie vibrating out of the home.

                        GORDON
            She ain't in on it.

                        CASTRO
            I have dreams about this, actual dreams
            about busting the top people, the rich
            people, the white people.

                        GORDON
            I'm telling you, she doesn't know shit.

                        CASTRO
            She knows Arnie Metzger.

                        GORDON
            So does half of San Diego.

                        CASTRO
            You want to make a wager on this?

A87 INT. STUDY - NIGHT   A87

The music is still playing. Helena looks numb. She motions
Arnie to her. He leans in.

                        HELENA
            If all our assets are frozen and our
            "sales force" has scattered... How am I
            supposed to survive? I'm giving birth in
            three months. How do I get through this?

                        ARNIE
            You're gonna get through it, but the
            first thing we do is get Michael Adler to
            represent Carl. We get Adler and we beat
            this thing.

                        HELENA
            How do I pay him?

                        ARNIE
            I suspect he'll accept his payment in
            publicity.

                                              CUT TO:

87   EXT. WAKEFIELD HOUSE - NIGHT   87

       A large, well-maintained Colonial on Mockingbird Valley Road,
       an upper-middle class neighborhood in the wealthy East End of
       Cincinnati. Leaves fall on the Saab wagon in the driveway.

88   INT. ROBERT'S STUDY - NIGHT   88

       Robert is looking at Caroline and he's not happy. Barbara is
       there, at a neutral distance from both of them.

                          ROBERT
              Caroline? How well did you know this boy
              who overdosed?

       She looks up beseechingly.

                          CAROLINE
              He didn't hang around us. He's like one
              of those hippie kids. I'm not part of
              that group. It was a party in all these
              rooms. His girlfriend who I barely know
              was completely hysterical... He's blue,
              he's puking... We didn't want to get in
              trouble, but what were we supposed to do?
                          (beat)
              I mean, what would you have done if you
              had been us?

                          BARBARA
              How well do you know this boy, Seth, who
              was driving? You know the police have
              charged him with a DUI and possession of
              marijuana.

                          CAROLINE
              He's a friend. He's also like the only
              one who was dealing with the situation.
              He'd definitely had a few beers, but it's
              not like he wanted to drive. We didn't
              know what else to do.
                          (beat)
              It wasn't *my* pot.

       She searches her parents' faces. It has been a convincing
       performance and she expects victory.

                          ROBERT
              Okay, honey. We understand. You're mother
              and I have to talk.

       Caroline is confused by this reaction.

                                                         (CONTINUED)

                         BARBARA
              Honey, we'd like to talk alone.

Caroline stands abruptly --

                         CAROLINE
              Like always.

Caroline leaves the study and shuts the door harder than
necessary.

Robert and Barbara look at each other, raising their eyebrows
and breathing deeply --

                         ROBERT
              I think she's lying.

                         BARBARA
              Me, too.

                         ROBERT
                   (reaching a decision)
              We'll ground her, clip her wings a bit.
              School and scheduled activities and
              that's it until further notice. This has
              to be handled delicately. Dan Kelly, in
              the District Attorney's office, will
              probably help us out, quietly. Christ,
              this could be embarrassing.

                         BARBARA
              Honey, this is difficult, but we've all
              had our moments. I tried --

                         ROBERT
              Stop. You experimented in college. I
              don't want to hear about that.

                         BARBARA
              Should we take the quotes off *experiment*
              and call it what it is?

                         ROBERT
              This is different.

                         BARBARA
              Why?

                         ROBERT
              To begin with, she's only sixteen years-
              old.

                                        (CONTINUED)

                              BARBARA
                    I think she has to find out for herself,
                    on her own. We have to allow her space --

                              ROBERT
                    Space for what? To O.D. like that other
                    kid? I will not send the message that
                    this type of behavior is okay with her
                    parents. Because it isn't. Correct?

                              BARBARA
                    We don't want to push her away. These are
                    growing experiences.

          Robert looks at his wife, then it dawns on him .

                              ROBERT
                    How long have you known about this?

          No response.

                              ROBERT (CONT'D)
                         (yelling)
                    How long have you known?

                              BARBARA
                    Six months. I found some marijuana,
                    that's all. And a little pipe about two
                    inches long. I talked with her. She said
                    her friends smoked pot and drank --

                              ROBERT
                    Explain to me how you could think that I
                    shouldn't know about this. Explain to me
                    how this wouldn't be relevant to me. As a
                    parent.

                              BARBARA
                    She asked me not to.

          He leaves the room.

89   INT. UPSTAIRS HALLWAY - NIGHT   89

          Robert is in the hallway, at Caroline's door. He opens it and
          we get BLASTED WITH MUSIC.

          Caroline is sitting in a rocking chair with headphones on.
          She faces the window and moves back and forth, back and
          forth.

          Robert calls her name, but the SOUNDTRACK is drowning him
          out.

                                                        (CONTINUED)

He calls again, this time apparently loud enough for her to
hear. She takes the headphones off - the MUSIC stops - and
turns to look at him. Or rather, she looks right through him,
as though he didn't exist. Robert is so taken aback by the
coldness of her gaze that he doesn't speak.

She turns away from him and puts the headphones back on.

                                                      CUT TO:

90   EXT. MILITARY BASE - MEXICO - DAY   90

Javier and Salazar walk across the base. Salazar is feeling
ebullient and it shows.

                         SALAZAR
              You watch and learn. I earn his trust.
              Then more pain. Then I appear with
              kindness. Within a week he will follow me
              around like a dog.

                         JAVIER
              But will he be house-trained?

                         SALAZAR
              When he loves me like a father, he will
              never tell anyone he was here. He will
              freely give the names of his superiors.
              Then we get them and they too will give
              us names. And eventually somebody will
              get us to Juan Obregon and the cartel
              will fall.

They enter the barracks.

91   INT. CELL - MEXICAN MILITARY BASE - DAY   91

It's pitch black in the cell. There's a human in here, but we
can't see him.

Suddenly the door is thrown open and light floods in,
illuminating a very broken Francisco Flores.

The figure of Commander Salazar fills the doorway.

                         SALAZAR
              This is shameful. A disgrace. Francisco
              Flores --

Francisco cowers in the corners --

                         SALAZAR (cont'd)
              It's all right, son. It's all right.
              Salazar is here.
                         (MORE)

                                                (CONTINUED)

                        SALAZAR (cont'd)
            You're among gentlemen, now. This
            shameful treatment will stop immediately.
                    (calling out)
            Guard!

A GUARD appears in the doorway. Francisco is spooked.

                        SALAZAR (cont'd)
            I want to know who is responsible for
            this treatment.

                        GUARD
            Yes, sir!

                        SALAZAR
            We aren't barbarians.

                        GUARD
            Yes, sir!

                        SALAZAR
            Bring this man a change of good clothes.
            Has he eaten?

                        GUARD
            I don't know, sir.

                        SALAZAR
                    (to Francisco)
            You will dine with me from now on.

Francisco moves closer to Salazar already feeling safe in his
presence.

                                                    CUT TO:

91   INT. COURTHOUSE, SAN DIEGO - DAY   92

A packed courthouse. Carl is at the defense table. He doesn't
look at Helena who sits in the gallery next to Arnie Metzger.

The PROSECUTOR is finishing his argument --

                        PROSECUTOR
            This is a man who heads a large criminal
            organization with international contacts
            we can only begin to understand. Our case
            against him is very strong. He is not a
            flight risk. His flight is assured. The
            people ask that your honor denies bail.

The prosecutor sits. Carl's defense lawyer, MICHAEL ADLER,
from the Georgetown party, stands and speaks.

                                                (CONTINUED)

> ADLER
> My client is no more a flight risk than
> your Honor or the able prosecutor. He is
> a pillar of his community, a family man
> with a wife and child in La Jolla, the
> community where he has made his home for
> over twenty years. As our defense will
> quickly show, my client is guilty of
> nothing more than being a handy target
> for an admitted criminal. Therefore we
> ask that you release Carl Ayala on his
> own recognizance.

Adler sits. The JUDGE makes a quick decision.

> JUDGE
> I'm gonna deny bail.

The judge SLAMS his gavel. The crowd is on its feet. Carl
tries to get a glimpse of Helena. They make eye contact.
Reporters from the press gallery are yelling for Helena.
Arnie ushers her away.

93   EXT. COURTHOUSE - DAY   93

Adler, Arnie, and Helena push through a crowd toward her car.
There are several reporters there who ask questions --

> REPORTER
> Mrs. Ayala, were you aware your husband
> is the largest cocaine smuggler in
> America?

> ADLER
> Alleged, people, alleged.

Helena gets into her car and slams the door. Adler faces the
reporters.

> REPORTER #2
> Mrs. Ayala is it true your husband has
> ordered a hit on Eduardo Ruiz?

Adler is in a role he relishes. Helena drives away. We move
up to Gordon, who is watching from the hotel window across
the street. He speaks into a walkie-talkie, and a car down
below pulls out to follow Helena.

> ADLER
> Carl Ayala sits on the board of the
> Children's Hospital. He is heavily
> involved with Adult Literacy. He has a
> small boy and another child on the way.
> (MORE)

                                                          (CONTINUED)

                              ADLER (cont'd)
                    If you spread this kind of innuendo, you
                    can expect legal recourse. Are we clear
                    on this point?

                                                              CUT TO:

94   INT. GOVERNMENT BUILDING - EARLY MORNING   94

      The marble government corridors are empty. No one is in yet.
      One office has lights on.

95   INT. A.D.A. KELLY'S OFFICE - EARLY MORNING   95

      Robert Wakefield talks with an Assistant District Attorney,
      DAN KELLY, 40's.

                              ROBERT
                    I appreciate you coming in so early.

                              A.D.A. KELLY
                    Judge Wakefield, it's an honor to handle
                    it for you. Consider it gone away. She's
                    a minor; it probably would've expunged on
                    her 18th birthday anyway.

                              ROBERT
                    Still, this was a sensitive issue for me
                    and I wanted to thank you personally.

                              A.D.A. KELLY
                    Like I said, open container, P.I.,
                    Misdemeanor possession. Easy to make it
                    disappear. For you, poof, it's gone.

      A.D.A Kelly thinks a moment, then tries for tact.

                              A.D.A. KELLY (cont'd)
                    One thing bothers me... That kid they
                    dropped off had coke *and* heroin in him.
                    Serious amounts. He's lucky he lived. So
                    I gotta ask: what's your daughter on?

                              ROBERT
                    I don't know what you mean.

                              A.D.A. KELLY
                    I mean, did you ask her? What kind of
                    drugs has she tried?

      Robert is silent for a beat.

                              ROBERT
                    I... I don't really know.

                                                          (CONTINUED)

> A.D.A. KELLY
> Is she in any kind of therapy...
> professional help?

> ROBERT
> No, of course not. She's one of the top
> students at her school.

> A.D.A. KELLY
> Well, I hope it stays that way.

96   INT. ROBERT'S CAR - EARLY MORNING   96

Robert in his car, thinking. The streets are empty. He picks
up the cell phone.

> ROBERT
> (into phone)
> It's Robert. Wipe our schedule clean for
> the next three days. I'm tired of talking
> to experts who never set foot outside the
> beltway. It's time to see the front
> lines.

97   INT. CAROLINE WAKEFIELD'S BATHROOM - MORNING   97

Caroline sits on the toilet in her private bathroom. She's
not going to the bathroom, it's a seat and she's wearing her
pajamas. She's reading a magazine. The exhaust fan is on.

There are pictures of her and her friends on the walls:
goofy photos from camp, from school, a collage she's made
with cutouts from magazine pictures and copy.

On the sink next to her is a little square of well-charred
aluminum foil; she's done many hits. She leans over and picks
up a small piece of crack cocaine from a small pile in her
soap dish. She drops it on a clean place on the foil. She
picks up a lighter and the tube of a ball point pen she's
turned into a straw.

She heats the bottom of the foil. The crack "crackles." She
chases the smoke across the foil. A huge hit. She leans her
head back, her eyes roll back, she tries to focus on the
magazine, on anything, she stares up at the ceiling. She
holds it as long as she can then blows it toward the exhaust
fan.

Caroline looks at her watch. It's 7:20. She stands suddenly,
unsteadily. She looks at herself in the mirror. She's really
high and indecisive. She looks around wildly. She sees the
shower. She turns it on. She drops her pajamas.

(CONTINUED)

She goes back to the foil and hits another piece of the rock,
taking another really big hit. She crushes the foil and
flushes it down the toilet. She hops in the shower.

98   IN THE SHOWER   98

The water streams over her face. After a long beat she
finally exhales the smoke of the hit through the water and
steam. She's in ecstacy.

It's almost time to leave for school.

                                                          CUT TO:

99   EXT. LA JOLLA PLAYGROUND - DAY   99

Helena reads a book, *Madame Bovary* by Gustave Flaubert, and
keeps an eye on David, who is playing on the monkey bars.

ACROSS THE ROAD at a careful distance is the ubiquitous
telephone repair van. On the roof a parabolic mike swivels
around.

100   INT. TELEPHONE REPAIR VAN - DAY   100

Castro and Gordon watch Helena via a small surveillance
monitor.

                    GORDON
          You should see little Montel play. Little
          Montel is the next Maradona.

                    CASTRO
          Maradona is a cokehead. Hand of God, my
          ass. We're wasting our time here.

                    GORDON
          He won. He was a winner. That bothers
          you.

                    CASTRO
          Winners don't do coke. Or haven't you
          been reading the bumper stickers?

Gordon looks at the monitor --

                    GORDON
          What do we have here?

ON THE MONITOR:

David kicking a soccer ball with an older strange man,
TIGRILLO, Latino, 40's, fit and tough looking.

                                                     (CONTINUED)

100   CONTINUED: 100

The man is very good. He juggles the ball and bounces it off
his head and David follows him away from the center of the
playground.

101   EXT. PLAYGROUND - CONTINUOUS   101

Helena notices David moving away while playing with the man.
She follows, then begins to jog after them.

                         HELENA
              David, come back here this minute. David!

As she closes distance the man stops juggling the ball and
abruptly picks up David and begins swinging him around by his
arms. David is having fun as Helena approaches.

                         HELENA (cont'd)
              David --

                         DAVID
              We're playing!

The strange man swings David up so that he's under his arm.

                         STRANGE MAN
              Yeah, this is fun.

                         HELENA
              Please put down my son.

The man holds David.

                         STRANGE MAN
              Shouldn't let your kid wander off with
              strangers.

                         HELENA
              Thank you. That's a valuable lesson.
              David, come on.

The strange man holds David tighter so that he's no longer
having fun. He begins to wriggle --

                         STRANGE MAN
              Mrs. Ayala --

This gets her attention --

                         STRANGE MAN (cont'd)
              Your husband owes a lot of money. Enough
              that snapping this kid's neck wouldn't
              nearly cover it.

David begins to cry. Helena looks around wildly for help.

                                                   (CONTINUED)

                          STRANGE MAN (cont'd)
                    You better come up with it in a hurry or
                    your kid is going to disappear, and he
                    won't turn up until the evening news.

He drops David who runs to his mother.

                          STRANGE MAN (cont'd)
                    You get exactly one warning.

The strange man moves away across the field.

                          STRANGE MAN (cont'd)
                    The first payment is three million
                    dollars.

He continues walking away.

102 INT. TELEPHONE REPAIR VAN - DAY   102

Gordon and Castro stare with rapt attention.

                          GORDON
                    Are you getting this on tape?

                          CASTRO
                    I love my job. I love it. The next time
                    I'm having a bad day you gotta remind me
                    of right now and I'll get over it.

                                                            CUT TO:

A103 EXT. BARRACKS - NIGHT   A103

Javier and Manolo stand guard outside the front door of the
dining hall. Javi smokes a cigarette.

                          MANOLO
                    A group of us are going out tonight.

                          JAVIER
                    Who?

                          MANOLO
                    Guzman, Tomas, Esteban --

                          JAVIER
                    Your new friends.

                          MANOLO
                    Yeah. It should be fun. You wanna come?

                                                      (CONTINUED)

                         JAVIER
               Not this time.

103 INT. DINING HALL - BARRACKS - NIGHT   103

     Francisco and Salazar eat at a beautifully set table. They
     are waited on by military officers who serve perfect flan at
     the end of the meal.

                         FRANCISCO
               In my home I have B&W speakers. I
               recently purchased a compact disc burner.
               I can make my own cd's, with whatever
               music I like, as if I bought them at the
               store, only I don't have to pay these
               crazy prices.

                         SALAZAR
               We have much in common. We both attended
               school in the United States, and both of
               our fathers are engineers.

                         FRANCISCO
               I got into stereo equipment when I was a
               kid. Some people don't notice the
               difference but it is very important to
               me.

                         SALAZAR
               Of course it is. Have some more wine.

     A soldier pours another glass of red for Francisco.

                         SALAZAR (cont'd)
               Now, Francisco, my friend... I must know
               where these men are who killed my
               captains. Not where they were last week,
               but where they are today, and better
               still, tomorrow. You are clever. You can
               predict where they will be, can't you?

     Francisco begins to weep.

     Salazar slides a pad of paper toward Francisco who slowly
     begins writing.

104 EXT. TIJUANA NEIGHBORHOOD - DAY   104

     Manolo and Javier pound on the front door of an apartment. A
     MAN opens the door and they grab him.

105   EXT. TIJUANA STREETS - DAY   105

A MAN walks down the street. Two SUV's pull up in front of
him. He starts to run. Salazar's men jump out and chase him.

Francisco is in the backseat of one of the SUV's, watching.

A106   EXT. TIJUANA - DAY   A106

An SUV pulls up to a curb.

B106   INT. SUV - DAY   B106

Javier and Manolo and Francisco sit in the SUV. Francisco is
weeping.

                    FRANCISCO
          I can't go home. I don't want to go.
          Please don't make me.

He looks beseechingly at them.

                    JAVIER
          It's not our decision.

                    FRANCISCO
          I'll be killed.

                    JAVIER
          Stop complaining. Nobody knows what
          you've been up to.

They push him out of the SUV.

                                                    CUT TO:

106   INT. SAN DIEGO JAIL - DAY   106

Castro and Gordon sit with Eduardo Ruiz in a conference room.
They are recording his statements.

                    RUIZ
          Carlos, I mean Carl, started out in the
          family connection business: real estate
          in Tijuana, fishing boats out of
          Ensenada, hydroponic raspberries. He met
          up with the Obregon brothers of the
          Tijuana Cartel who were interested in two
          things: entering society and using his
          fishing boats.

                    GORDON
          So you pay off our customs officials?

                                              (CONTINUED)

> RUIZ
> In Mexico law enforcement is an
> entrepreneurial activity, this is not so
> true for the USA.
> (condescending)
> Using regression analysis we made a study
> of the customs lanes at the border and
> calculated the odds of a search. The odds
> are not high, and we found variables that
> reduce the odds. We hire drivers with
> nothing to lose. Then we throw a lot of
> product at the problem. Some get stopped.
> Enough get through. It's not difficult.

> CASTRO
> You'd think he wasn't sitting here facing
> life in prison.

> RUIZ
> This has worked for years and it will
> continue to work for years. NAFTA makes
> everything more difficult for you. The
> border is disappearing.
> (pointing at them)
> You people are like those Japanese
> soldiers left behind on deserted islands
> who think that World War II is still
> going on.
> (with total disdain)
> Let me be the first to tell you, your
> government surrendered this war a long
> time ago.

> GORDON
> (to Castro)
> This attitude's not gonna help him any,
> is it?

> RUIZ
> I got greedy. I decided to bring a little
> in on my own and somebody tipped you off.
> That was my mistake. Carl would never be
> so stupid.

> GORDON
> He hired you. That was a mistake.

> RUIZ
> Carl and I were friends from childhood.
> He was loyal, that's not a mistake.

107 EXT. TIJUANA - SAN DIEGO BORDER CROSSING - DAY   107

Car after car, an unending multi-lane stream of vehicles
moving into the U.S. Any of these cars could be carrying
drugs.

108 INT. CUSTOMS CONTROL BOOTH - DAY   108

On an elevated walkway, this booth commands a view of
everything. Robert and Sheridan listen to an OFFICIAL give
the spiel.

                         OFFICIAL
              The busiest land border crossing in the
              world. Over forty-one thousand vehicles
              per day, twenty-two thousand pedestrians
              on foot. I think we do a pretty good job
              but we know a lot of drugs are still
              getting through.

                         ROBERT
              Any idea how much?

                         OFFICIAL
              I've read official estimates but I
              wouldn't bet my house on them. I've heard
              the entire cocaine supply for the United
              States can fit into four tractor-
              trailers.
                   (gestures to the traffic)
              At least a half-dozen of those cars right
              out there are carrying a load of dope,
              with drivers employed by people who don't
              give a damn if they're caught or not.

                         ROBERT
              What do you look for?

                         OFFICIAL
              We ask questions and measure the answers.
              When something doesn't ring true, a fact
              that doesn't make sense, a slight
              hesitation, then it's off to secondary
              for a closer look. Before NAFTA we had
              about 1.9 million trucks a year. Now it's
              almost double. Pretty soon there'll be
              Mexican truck companies that will have as
              much freedom in crossing the border as
              American truck companies.

                         ROBERT
              Any way we can do it better?

                                              (CONTINUED)

                        OFFICIAL
              Sure. More money in intelligence on their
              side of the border. So we have a better
              idea who we're looking for. More dogs.
              More people. Supposed to be getting some
              giant x-ray machines to run the trucks
              through. Outside of martial law that's
              about the best you're gonna do.
                (beat)
              But, I should tell you, there are two
              things that really have us on edge right
              now.
                (beat)
              In the last six month seizures have
              tripled, even though we're pulling over
              the same number of cars. What does that
              tell you?

                        ROBERT
              That triple the amount of stuff is going
              through.

                        OFFICIAL
              Right. But, that's not the biggest
              problem. One of our Intel officers picked
              up information from DEA that traffickers
              have come up with a process, a chemical
              process, to turn coke into something
              else. It doesn't smell like coke. It
              doesn't look like coke. And what's worse,
              it doesn't react to field test. It could
              be anything. Maybe it's already
              happening. I mean, how would we know?

Robert looks out at the border activity. It's anarchy.

                                          CUT TO:

109 INT. AYALA STUDY - AFTERNOON   109

Helena is on the floor surrounded by papers. She's made piles
of certain things: articles of incorporation,
shipping/transfer documentation, bank statements, credit card
statements. She holds a telephone to her ear --

                        HELENA
                (into phone)
              Yes, hi Jenny, account number 4168 2245
              3173... I need a cash advance.

Helena walks into her kitchen. It's serene in the afternoon
light. She fixes ice-cold lemonade and fills two plastic
cups.

                                        (CONTINUED)

>   HELENA (cont'd)
>   What's the largest amount I can get?
>   (listens)
>   Okay, I guess that'll have to do.

Helena hangs up the phone. She takes the two cups of
lemonade to the front door and steps outside.

110   EXT. AYALA HOME - AFTERNOON   110

Helena carries the cups down the driveway. She presses a
button and the gates swing open.

111   INT. TELEPHONE REPAIR VAN - AFTERNOON   111

Gordon and Castro listen to their headsets. Suddenly --

>   VOICE (O.S.)
>   (over their headsets)
>   Okay. She's coming out. She's leaving her
>   property. Okay, she seems to be heading
>   for the van! She is approaching the van!

Castro and Gordon look at each other.

>   GORDON
>   What do we do?

>   CASTRO
>   I don't know.

There's a KNOCKING at the door of the van.

>   GORDON
>   What do you think she wants?

>   CASTRO
>   She's your girlfriend. Open it, talk
>   about your kids.

Gordon opens the door. Helena is standing there with the
lemonade.

>   HELENA
>   I so hope I didn't startle you. I thought
>   you might like some cold lemonade.

>   GORDON
>   Uh... Thank you.

She hands the cups to him. Helena gathers herself.

(CONTINUED)

111 CONTINUED: 111

                              HELENA
               I know this is a difficult situation and
               you're only doing your jobs. I don't bear
               you any ill-will, but I do have a small
               favor to ask.

                              CASTRO
               You want to ask us a favor?

                              HELENA
               A man threatened my children. These
               charges have attracted a lot of attention
               and it seems to be bringing all the nut-
               jobs out of the nut jar.
                         (beat)
               Would you keep an eye out for anything
               out of the ordinary. I don't know what
               else to do.

                              GORDON
               Of course, we will.

                              HELENA
               Thank you.

     They shut the door to the van and sit for a moment.

                              CASTRO
               It's probably poisoned.

     Gordon takes a big sip of his.

                              GORDON
               It's good. Not too sweet.

                                                              CUT TO:

112 OMITTED   112

113 OMITTED   113

114 OMITTED   114

A115 EXT. TIJUANA STREET - MORNING   A115

     This is a questionable neighborhood pushed up against the
     edge of poverty.

     Anna hurries across the street.

B115 EXT. JAVI'S APARTMENT BUILDING - MORNING   B115

    Anna walks up the stairs of a rundown building. She passes
    two PROSTITUTES loitering in the stairwell.

    She knocks on a door and Javi, half-dressed for work,
    answers. He's surprised to see her.

                    JAVIER
          Anna. What's wrong? What do you want?

                    ANNA
          I can't find Manolo.

                    JAVIER
          He's not here.

                    ANNA
          He never came home last night. Was he
          with you?

                    JAVIER
              No.

    He lets her into the apartment.

C115 INT. JAVI'S APARTMENT - MORNING   C115

    A small, clean room with a partition for the sleeping area.

                    ANNA
          I'm worried. Last time he was out late,
          I went through his clothes while he was
          asleep.

    She pulls out a plastic packet with the scorpion insignia and
    911 stamped on it.

    Javier thinks a beat.

                    JAVIER
          I'll find him.

D115 EXT. ALLEY - TIJUANA - DAY   D115

    Javi slams Manolo against the side of building.

                    JAVIER
          What the fuck are you doing? You're
          supposed to be at work. Look at you.

    Manolo is sweaty and crazy-eyed.

                                        (CONTINUED)

> MANOLO
> It's no problem. I was just with
> everybody we work with.

> JAVIER
> Oh, really. General Salazar was there?

> MANOLO
> No, but a lot of other people. You should
> come. You should come out with us.

> JAVIER
> Go home. Get cleaned up. Get to work.
> Salazar is heading down to Mexico City
> next week and I'm not getting left
> behind. Don't fuck this up.

                                                  CUT TO:

EXT. COFFEE KIOSK - TIJUANA - DAY

Javi buys a cup of coffee. He turns. Two men, who will come
to be known as AGENT HUGHES and AGENT JOHNSON, are standing
close. Agent Hughes speaks without looking at him.

> HUGHES
> The word going around is you're not that
> happy in your work.
>   (beat)
> Maybe we can help.

Hughes sticks a business card in Javi's pocket. Javi watches
them walk away. It's all done so smoothly and quickly, it's
over before Javi even knows what happened.

115 EXT. WEST END - CINCINNATI - DAY   115

It's the bad part of urban Cincinnati in the daylight:
projects and blighted row houses. Seth and Caroline walk with
a slouched, alert air. In their mind's eye they are prep-
school gangsters following a familiar route.

> SETH
> You know my dad takes eight red cold
> pills every day? He and my mom have
> cocktail hour every night, from six to
> seven, set your clock, two bourbons --

> CAROLINE
> Maybe we could show up and smoke a little
> rock with them to unwind --

                                             (CONTINUED)

                    SETH
          Yeah, then some dope to take the edge off
          at the end of a long day.

                    CAROLINE
          Have you done your homework, honey?

                    SETH
          Yes, mom --

                    CAROLINE
          Then here's a little bump.

They turn down a street with a lot of activity on it.

                    SETH
          Drugs weren't even a problem until a
          hundred years ago when the white men in
          power declared them a problem. Opiates.
          But, who was using 'em? Chinese
          immigrants. Slave labor. And the *darkies*
          up in the inner cities dancing to them
          evil rhythms of ju-ju music. People on
          the fringe. Artists. *Decadent* rich
          people. And who got scared? White men in
          power. Who's scared today? White men in
          power. If J.P. Morgan and John D.
          Rockefeller ever admitted using, it'd be
          a whole different story.

TWO YOUNG STREET DEALERS fall in step with them. One talks
without moving his lips --

                    STREET DEALER
          What you want?

                    SETH
          911, and the come down.

One dealer hurries ahead toward the doorway of a falling-down
building.

                    STREET DEALER
          How much?

                    SETH
          Two hundred of C, hundred of the other.

The dealer looks them over. He looks behind them down the
street.

                    CAROLINE
          Come on... We've been here before.

                                              (CONTINUED)

                         STREET DEALER
                   Then, let's see your money.

Seth and Caroline are suspicious. They carefully show money
they both have in their front right pockets. The dealer
feints like he might grab it.

                         STREET DEALER (cont'd)
                   Up the steps. You the experts. You know
                   what to do.

They hurry up the steps into the dingy brownstone.

116 INT. ROW HOUSE - DAY   116

They step into the narrow foyer between the outer door and
the inner door. There are three other PEOPLE waiting
nervously. An older JUNKIE shoots them a crazy look --

                         JUNKIE
                   What are you two, about twelve?

                         CAROLINE
                   Fuck off.

They wait. Finally, the first dealer appears in the inner
door and lets them through.

117 INT. FIRST FLOOR CORRIDOR - DAY   117

They wait in a line in the narrow, poorly lit corridor. At
the end of the hall a hatch in a door slides back and the
drugstore is open. People buy and leave.

Seth and Caroline approach. In the hatch is a hardened
dealer, 20's, named SKETCH, which is tattooed on his forearm.
He checks out Caroline's body.

                         SETH
                   Caroline, give me your money.

She hands over her money to Seth who pays and gets the drugs:
gram baggies of rock stamped with a scorpion and "911," and
wax-paper bindles of heroin, also labeled, "911."

Caroline has been watching the transaction. Sketch makes slow
eye contact with Caroline. After a beat --

                         SKETCH
                   Goodbye... Caroline.

Seth and Caroline make their way out of the building.

                                                          (CONTINUED)

                              SETH
                        (under his breath)
                    Yeah, right.

118 EXT. BUILDING - DAY   118

     Seth and Caroline hold hands as they hurry down the steps.
     The lookout speaks without moving his lips.

                         STREET DEALER
                    Now, get the fuck out of here.

     Caroline stops suddenly. She pulls Seth to her and kisses him
     hard. There's no better moment than the one right after
     scoring before you start using.

119 EXT. VILLA ELAINE - DAY   119

     A flophouse of the seediest variety: wino in the doorway,
     prostitutes taking care of business, everyone fresh out of
     institutions and graveyards.

120 INT. VILLA ELAINE - DAY   120

     They approach the front desk which is behind six inches of
     glass.

                              SETH
                    We'd like room 205.

                            DESKMAN
                    Then you hand me twenty-eight dollars.

121 INT. ROOM 205 - VILLA ELAINE - DAY   121

     They enter and the light bulb goes out. Seth fumbles his way
     to the mini-fridge, which he opens, throwing feeble light
     across the floor.

     They check out the decrepit room: the sloping mattress, the
     black and white television bolted to the bureau. The mini-
     fridge. Caroline bounces on the bed. They are teenagers. Seth
     prepares the drugs by the light of the mini-fridge.

                              SETH
                    I love this place.

     Seth dumps the drugs on the bedside table. From other pockets
     he extracts aluminum foil, lighter, tube. She trails away
     watching him fix the first hit.

                                                       (CONTINUED)

                         SETH (CONT'D)
               Did Courtney Love play Nancy in Syd and
               Nancy?

                         CAROLINE
               I think so. If she didn't she should
               have.
                    (checks her watch)
               I've only got maybe an hour. Then
               volleyball practice is over and I have to
               be home.

                         SETH
               Why? Nobody's there.

He prepares the first hit. She does it and lies back. He does
one.

                         CAROLINE
                    (blowing out the hit)
               The maid... They ask her what time I get
               back. She spies for them.

Seth starts kissing her. They try to get into it, but both of
them are thinking about the drugs.

                         CAROLINE (cont'd)
               I wish we could stay here. Just be here
               forever and ever. Make it a little home.

She leans over to snort a tiny line of heroin.

                         SETH
               I want to have sex and do a hit right as
               we're coming.

Caroline's distracted by the line she's snorting. After a
while...

                         CAROLINE
               Okay.

Seth begins undoing her jeans.

                                                     CUT TO:

122 INT. EPIC BUNKER LOBBY - DAY   122
     SUPERTITLE: EL PASO, TEXAS

     Robert and Sheridan listen to the official tour of the EPIC
     center delivered by the SPECIAL-AGENT-IN-CHARGE, 40, a
     sincere weight-lifter with a sincere crew-cut.

                                                     (CONTINUED)

>   SPECIAL-AGENT-IN-CHARGE
>   ... Over 200 DEA field agents, a budget
>   of almost 100 million dollars and state
>   of the art communications equipment make
>   the El Paso Information Center the Drug
>   Enforcement Administration's flagship for
>   the 21st century.

123   INT. EPIC BUNKER CAFETERIA - DAY   123

A huge lunchroom. Long plastic institutional tables and
agents minding their own business.

Robert, Sheridan, and their Epic Guide walk through. They
pass a wall of black and white head shots --

>   ROBERT
>   Who are these guys?

>   SPECIAL-AGENT-IN-CHARGE
>   Agents who died in the field.

124   EXT. BINOCULAR POV - DAY   124

of a large mansion with manicured grounds. The back lawn is
filled with children, balloons, a merry-go-round, and pony
rides. It's a sumptuous children's birthday party.

>   SPECIAL-AGENT-IN-CHARGE
>   That house, that you see from the DEA
>   headquarters, belonged to Porfirio
>   Madrigal -- the Lord of the Skies,
>   largest trafficker in Mexico.

ANGLE ON ROBERT

looking through the binoculars.

>   ROBERT
>   He died in a liposuction surgery, right?

>   SPECIAL-AGENT-IN-CHARGE
>   Right. Now it's used by somebody from the
>   Juarez Cartel, one of his lieutenants...
>   Who knows?
>   (beat)
>   Every damn day there's a birthday party.
>   At first I thought they must have three
>   hundred children, then I realized they're
>   taunting us. Three miles away and we
>   can't touch them. Ha, ha, ha.

                                                         (CONTINUED)

BINOCULAR POV: a child running in circles holding a clutch of
colored balloons.

> ROBERT
> Who do we interface with on their side?

> SPECIAL-AGENT-IN-CHARGE
> What do you mean?

> ROBERT
> I mean, who runs interdiction on the
> Mexico side?

> SPECIAL-AGENT-IN-CHARGE
> I don't know. I don't think there's any
> one person.
>   (thinks)
> See the problem is the Juarez cartel owns
> everything and everybody, all the
> property on the Mexican side, sometimes
> all the property on both sides.
> Warehouses, transportation, even tunnels.
> It's very organized.

125   EXT. TARMAC - DAY   125

Robert, walking with purpose, leads his group to their plane.

126   INT. MILITARY JET - DAY   126

Robert and Sheridan and several DEA, Law Enforcement, and
Military Officials. It's a nice plane, used for important
people and Robert has the best seat.

> ROBERT
> I want everyone thinking out the box for
> a second. What are we gonna do about
> Mexico?
>   (silence)
> Come on, guys. Out of the box.

The men on the plane just stare at him. Finally the REP FROM
DEA leans forward.

> REP FROM DEA
> Unlimited funds?

> ROBERT
> Unlimited.

> REP FROM DEA
> From a DEA standpoint we need a vetted
> task force and matching funds.
>   (MORE)

(CONTINUED)

                              REP FROM DEA (cont'd)
                    And cut the red tape on getting them
                    equipment and training.

          Robert turns to the others.

                              ROBERT
                    Come on. I want to hear from everyone:
                    FBI. Customs. Treatment. Is there anyone
                    from treatment on this plane?
                         (no one answers)
                    Then I want an answer for why there isn't
                    anyone from treatment.
                         (beat)
                    Look, we know we have to bust one of
                    these cartels, Juarez or Tijuana, not
                    just as a symbol, but hell yes, also as a
                    symbol - they are symbols - and there's
                    nothing wrong with sending a message.
                    That's why when Carlos Ayala hired
                    Michael Adler lead defense, I flew Ben
                    Williams to San Diego to prosecute.
                    Because he's the best we have, he's our
                    symbol that we're serious about putting
                    the top people away.
                         (beat)
                    So, as of right now, this flight only,
                    consider the dam on new ideas thrown
                    open.

          Still, no one else says anything. They watch Robert
          impassively.

                              ROBERT (cont'd)
                    If I'm not mistaken, we got DEA,
                    Pentagon, U.S. Attorneys office, about a
                    billion dollars of budget right here. So
                    what are you people waiting for?

                                                          CUT TO:

127 OMITTED   127

128 EXT. SAN DIEGO OFFICE BUILDING - DAY   128

          Establishing shot of a tall glass building in the downtown
          skyline of San Diego.

129 INT. ARNIE METZGER'S OFFICE - DAY   129

          Helena and Arnie enter his office. The furniture is sleek mid-
          century modern, and the view of the harbor is extraordinary.

                              ARNIE
                    On a clear day you can see Mexico City.

                                                          (CONTINUED)

Arnie stands very close to Helena and looks at her profile.

                    ARNIE (cont'd)
          This place is swept twice a day. I
          learned that in Miami in '85. Then the
          U.S. shut down the whole Caribbean, but
          it's a big game of wack-a-mole. Knock it
          down in Miami, it pops up here. And San
          Diego is so much more relaxing.

                    HELENA
          Arnie, I need money. Somebody threatened
          my children. They want a first payment of
          three million dollars.

                    ARNIE
          Helena, if I had it I would give it to
          you, but I don't have that kind of money.

                    HELENA
          Arnie, help me. Doesn't anyone owe us
          money?

                    ARNIE
          Yes, I told you before, there are people
          who owe you money but they're not paying.
          There's too much heat on Carl.

                    HELENA
          Please. Tell me who Carl sells to.

Arnie thinks.

                    ARNIE
          Even if I knew I wouldn't tell you. You
          do not want to come into contact with
          these people. Only Carl knows who they
          are. That's his real asset. Ruiz doesn't
          know them. They don't know Ruiz. Church
          and State.

                    HELENA
          What about legitimate businesses? We own
          a construction concern, real estate --

                    ARNIE
          Laundromats for the washing of money.
          Unfortunately, Carl had only one
          successful business.

                    HELENA
          Don't you have some good news? Isn't
          there something positive you could say.

                                        (CONTINUED)

8

There isn't. Helena looks Arnie in the eyes.

                    HELENA (CONT'D)
               (vulnerable)
          Sometimes I wonder what I'll do if Carl
          doesn't get out. I'm not very adept at
          being on my own. I've always had a man in
          my life. Always.

                    ARNIE
          I remember when I first met you: little
          Helen Watts from the wrong side of
          somewhere. I had a feeling even then that
          your survival instincts were pretty well
          honed.

                    HELENA
          I'm glad you think so, but I'm picturing
          a debt-ridden, thirty-two year-old mother
          whose ex-husband is being compared to
          Pablo Escobar.
               (beat)
          And I'm wondering who would want to be
          with someone like that?

It takes a great effort for Arnie not to answer.

                                                       CUT TO:

A130 OMITTED   A130

131   OMITTED   131

132   OMITTED   132

133   OMITTED   133

134   OMITTED   134

A135 INT. ARMORED SUV - MEXICO - DAY   A135

     Javier and Manolo ride through a nice neighborhood in Mexico
     City. Javi isn't familiar with the roads and drives
     cautiously.

     A young lady, ROSARIO, early 20's, sexy and vulnerable, rides
     in the back of the SUV.

                    ROSARIO
          You two don't like me, do you?

     Manolo laughs and looks her up and down. Javi watches her in
     the rearview mirror.

                                                   (CONTINUED)

A135 CONTINUED: A135

                          JAVIER
              We don't have an opinion on you.

                          ROSARIO
                      (to Javi)
              Maybe it's because I'm getting an
              apartment nicer than anything you'll ever
              see in your life?

Javi says nothing.

                          ROSARIO (cont'd)
                      (re: the neighborhood)
              I can't believe the old man kept his
              promise.

                          JAVIER
              The General is a man of his word.

                          ROSARIO
              They will say anything to get what they
              want, but then you remind them, it's
              always tomorrow, tomorrow, tomorrow.
                      (beat)
              Occupational hazard, I guess.

Javi just looks at her in the rearview mirror.

                          ROSARIO (CONT'D)
              His friend is giving us the apartment so
              it's not like he paid. It's more like a
              favor.

Javier pulls the SUV to the curb in front of a beautiful
colonial-style apartment complex in the verdant neighborhood.

B135 EXT. VERDANT NEIGHBORHOOD - DAY   B135

Birds are chirping. Javi waits in the car as Manolo takes the
young lady's bags from the vehicle and carries them up the
walkway to the arched doorway. He knocks on the heavy wooden
door.

                          ROSARIO
              You don't have the keys. Oh that's
              perfect. Are you an idiot?

Manolo knocks again. They wait a long beat.

                          MANOLO
              There's supposed to be someone here to
              let you in.

                                                      (CONTINUED)

B135 CONTINUED: B135

        Finally, the door swings open and a BODYGUARD is standing
        there. Rosario SQUEALS and sweeps past him into the vast
        space. The bodyguard motions for Manolo to put the bags
        inside the door.

        Manolo sets the bags down and sees another MAN standing a few
        feet away. The man wears sunglasses. His complexion is
        strange and his neck is bandaged.

        The body guard escorts Manolo back outside where he hears
        Rosario's happy LAUGHTER drifting down from an upstairs
        window.

C135 INT. SUV - DAY   C135

        Manolo gets into the truck. He's shaken by what he's just
        seen.

                        MANOLO
                Madrigal's alive.

                        JAVIER
                What?

                        MANOLO
                Porfirio Madrigal is not dead. I just saw
                him.

        A long beat as Javier considers this.

                        JAVIER
                This is why Salazar is so interested in
                cleaning up Tijuana. Madrigal, who's
                supposed to be dead, owns him. And
                Madrigal is making a move on Juan
                Obregon.

        Javier calmly drives away.

                        MANOLO
                Javi! Come on. Don't pull this you don't
                care bullshit. This is incredible
                information. It must be. Javi --

                        JAVIER
                We keep our mouths shut.

                                                  CUT TO:

135   INT. BARBARA'S CAR - NIGHT   135

        Barbara drives Robert home from the airport. There's a sense
        they've been silent for a while.

                                                  (CONTINUED)

              ROBERT
     I think we may have found our Mexican
     Drug Czar. It's this General, Salazar. At
     least I'll have somebody on the other
     side I can talk to.

              BARBARA
     Does this mean you're going to be gone
     more?

A long silence.

              ROBERT
     Possibly.

Another silence.

              BARBARA
     You might want to pencil in a little *face-
     time* with your daughter.

              ROBERT
     Barbara --

              BARBARA
     Because I'm at the edge of my
     capabilities, Robert.

              ROBERT
     The first thing we have to do is present
     a unified front.

              BARBARA
     If you start in on the war metaphors I'm
     going to drive this car into a fucking
     telephone pole.

              ROBERT
     Look, I'm as worried as you are --

              BARBARA
     No, I don't think so. *Leave me alone,
     give me money.* That's what I get from our
     daughter. She has a way of shutting me
     out that seems very familiar.

              ROBERT
     Yeah, well, she has a way of self-
     medicating that probably seems familiar,
     too.

She looks at him, stung.

                                        (CONTINUED)

                              BARBARA
                    I'm not the one who has to have three
                    scotches just to walk in the door and say
                    hello.

                              ROBERT
                    I have a drink before dinner to take the
                    edge off my day. That's different.

                              BARBARA
                    Oh, it is?

                              ROBERT
                    Yeah, because the alternative is to be
                    bored to death.

136   EXT. WAKEFIELD HOUSE - NIGHT   136

      The car pulls into the driveway. Robert gets out. Barbara
      doesn't. He looks back at her.

                              BARBARA
                    Why don't you go in and tell your
                    daughter how bored you are.

      She puts the car in reverse and drives away. He stands for a
      moment, steaming.

137   INT. WAKEFIELD HOUSE - NIGHT   137

      Robert Wakefield steps inside his home. It's very QUIET. He
      checks the mail on the hall table.

138   INT. UPSTAIRS HALLWAY - NIGHT   138

      Robert walks down the hallway. He steps into Caroline's
      bedroom.

139   INT. CAROLINE WAKEFIELD'S BEDROOM - CONTINUOUS   139

      Robert stands outside her closed bathroom door.

      There is nothing, then from the other side of the door, the
      faint sound of a lighter CLICKING. AGAIN and AGAIN, then a
      COUGH.

140   INT. CAROLINE WAKEFIELD'S BATHROOM - NIGHT   140

      Caroline sits on the toilet. Glamour Magazine on her lap.
      She's wild-eyed and paranoid. The exhaust fan is running. The
      aluminum foil is on the sink. The last little bit of heroin
      in a wax-paper bundle sits beside it.

                                                            (CONTINUED)

She's listening hard for any SOUND in the house. What she's
wondering is if someone is outside the door listening.

She puts a piece of crack on the foil and listens hard once
more before lighting it. She does the hit. And seems to feel
better.

Suddenly there's a POUNDING on the door. The VOICE of her
father muffled through the solid wood.

                    ROBERT (V.O.)
                (muffled by the door)
            Caroline. Open this door immediately.

Caroline is up like a shot. She looks around. The POUNDING on
the door gets stronger.

She crumples the foil and drops it in the toilet.

The bathroom door SOUNDS like it's about to cave inward.

                    CAROLINE
                (faking the best she can)
            Who is it? I'm going to the bathroom.

She's coping now, full parallel process mode: she dumps the
last heroin on the back of her hand and snorts it, checking
her nose in the mirror as she reaches for a can of air
freshener which she sprays into the air.

                    CAROLINE (cont'd)
            One minute.

She takes the remaining crack, lighters, tubes, little smudgy
druggy bits of paraphernalia and carefully places it all in a
hiding place above the bathroom cabinet.

She pauses a beat, then opens the door, and tries to brush by
her father while avoiding his eyes.

                    CAROLINE (cont'd)
            Excuse me --

Robert grabs her by the arms. He pushes her against the wall
and looks at her pupils. He looks at her fingernails. The
blister on her thumb from working the lighter is red and
irritated.

                    ROBERT
            You're not going anywhere, young lady.

She stands there; she's very high.

                                              (CONTINUED)

Robert sniffs the air. He throws open cabinets, searching for drugs. He sees the smudge mark on the counter left by the charred aluminum foil.

> ROBERT (cont'd)
> Where is it? Where are the drugs?
> (yelling)
> Where are they?

> CAROLINE
> Fuck you. I wasn't doing anything.
> You're like the Gestapo.

Robert KICKS the cabinets.

> ROBERT
> Fuck me? Oh, okay. Fuck me. Fuck you.

Robert is losing it. He throws stuff around the bathroom

and then, for the first time, looks up. He sees the long light in the box atop the medicine cabinet and it dawns on him.

> ROBERT (cont'd)
> I'm going to ask you one time to tell me
> the truth so that I can help you.

She just stares.

> ROBERT (CONT'D)
> Okay, young lady, that's it.

> CAROLINE
> Like I give a fuck.

Robert reaches above the medicine cabinet and pulls out a charred spoon. It confuses him. He throws it into the sink.

He pulls out another spoon. He pulls out crumpled bindles, rolled up, encrusted dollar bills, exhausted lighters, a pill bottle, an empty pint of vodka.

The detritus of drug addiction keeps on coming, filling up the sink. Robert stares at it, the amount and complexity has him momentarily baffled.

> ROBERT
> What is wrong with you? What?
> (beat)
> You're going away. You're getting help
> somewhere.

(CONTINUED)

                        CAROLINE
            You can't make me.

                        ROBERT
            Oh, yes I can.

                                                        CUT TO:

141   OMITTED   141

142   OMITTED   142

143   OMITTED   143

A144 INT. - SAN DIEGO - DAY   A144

      Javier drives toward downtown. He's sipping a Burger King
      soft-drink. On the seat next to him is a shopping bag from
      Target. He takes an exit. Javier pulls into the underground
      parking lot of a fancy office tower.

B144 INT. POLICE SEDAN - DAY   B144

      Javi drives down to the third floor underground. He pulls
      into a parking spot next to a white sedan. He slides open the
      cargo door of his van.

      The cargo door of the sedan opens. Javi quickly gets into the
      sedan.

C144 INT. SEDAN - DAY   C144

      Special Agents Hughes and Johnson welcome Javi.

                        JAVIER
            Where are we going?

      Hughes sticks out his hand.

                        HUGHES
            Special Agent Hughes, Drug Enforcement
            Administration of the United States.

                        JAVIER
                  (ignoring the niceties)
            Where are you taking me?

      The agents exchange a look.

                        JOHNSON
            Somewhere safe.

                                              (CONTINUED)

                         JAVIER
          Where?

                         JOHNSON
          A place we have, that we know is
          protected.

                         JAVIER
          No.

                         HUGHES
          It's really safe.

                         JAVIER
          Not for me.

                         JOHNSON
          Okay. Where would you like to go?

D144 EXT. SWIMMING POOL - HOTEL - DAY   D144

     Javi and Agents Johnson and Hughes stand in the middle of the
     shallow end of a large swimming pool. KIDS in waterwings
     splash nearby.

                         JAVIER
          It's important that we work together.
          Mexico. America. One hand washing the
          other.

                         JOHNSON
          We agree.

                         JAVIER
          So... maybe you tell me about your
          informants in our operations.

                         JOHNSON
              (confused by this)
          We thought maybe you'd have that kind of
          information for us.

                         JAVIER
              (feigning surprise)
          This is a very different proposition.

     Johnson and Hughes exchange a glance.

                         JOHNSON
          We pay for that kind of information.

     A fat kid in an inner-tube floats behind them.

                                                    (CONTINUED)

D144 CONTINUED: D144

                    JOHNSON (CONT'D)
          Is that what you're talking about,
          Javier?

Javi makes eye contact with one agent, then the other.

                    JAVIER
          Ten years ago Tijuana had no drug
          problem. Now it is epidemic.
                    (beat)
          Ten years ago America takes a hammer to
          Pablo Escobar, a hammer to the Miami drug
          trade, and you allowed everything to move
          to my country. You dumped the problem at
          our feet. Now, drug use is epidemic. Now,
          the treatment centers are full and get no
          state money. They survive on donations
          and what they get for building doghouses
          to sell to the U.S.
                    (beat)
          We need lights for the parks so kids can
          play at night. So they can play baseball.
          So it's safe. Everybody likes parks.
          Everybody likes baseball.
                    (beat)
          What I'm talking about is I would like to
          see somebody take an interest in Tijuana.
          That's what I'm talking about.

Javi starts to get out of the pool.

                    HUGHES
          Javi, You want to come see us again,
          you're going on the box. No more of this
          water-wing bullshit.

E144 INT. PARKING GARAGE - DAY   E144

    Javier gets out of the DEA sedan and back into his. He drives
    away.

F144 INT. SEDAN - DAY   F144

    Agent Hughes turns to Agent Johnson.

                    JOHNSON
          You wanna tell me what the hell that was
          all about?

                                        (CONTINUED)

                    HUGHES
          He's got something. We just have to be
          patient.

                                                      CUT TO:

144   INT. JAIL VISITATION ROOM - DAY   144

      Helena and Carl each hold a telephone receiver as they stare
      at each other through a thick pane of meshed glass. Helena is
      barely holding it together. It's hard for Carl to see her
      like this. After a beat --

                    CARL
          How's David?

                    HELENA
          How's David? *How's David*? He's terrific,
          Carl.

                    CARL
          Helena --

                    HELENA
          He watched his father get dragged away by
          federal agents. I don't even know how to
          begin to tell him where you are or when
          you're coming back... Or if you're coming
          back.

      She can't even look at him.

                    CARL
               (beat)
          We'll get through this, I promise. I'll
          make it up to you --

                    HELENA
               (snapping)
          How? Supportive letters from prison while
          I'm being kicked out of our home?
               (beat)
          Do you have any idea what is happening
          out here? Our credit cards are maxed. The
          people at the bank, you should see their
          faces when I walk in there. I have a
          letter from the government telling me
          that anything I sell from our house will
          be taken against an income tax lien. Our
          friends are behaving like the crowd at a
          public hanging. Nobody will help us.
          Nobody will take us in. Nobody wants
          anything to do with us.
               (MORE)

                                                   (CONTINUED)

> HELENA (cont'd)
> So tell me, Carl, how you're gonna make
> it up to me.
>   (losing it)
> Tell me again how we'll get through this,
> and maybe while you're at it you can put
> your hand up against the glass so we can
> have a tender moment of connection.

> CARL
> Helena --

> HELENA
> Tell me what to do, Carl. I need
> guidance, not a fucking platitude.
>   (beat)
> I'm not bringing a child into the kind of
> life I grew up with. I won't do it. I
> want our life back.

Carl looks at his wife as if he is trying to weigh her. He
thinks, then leans forward --

> CARLOS
> I built our house and I don't want to
> lose it. Every stone, every brick, every
> board.
>   (carefully)
> My business... That would take a lot of
> private study...
>   (he blinks)
> That you don't have time for. I suggest
> you look into the Coronel...
>   (he blinks again)
> Into selling it. If you can stomach it,
> you should look into it. That painting is
> very valuable.

> HELENA
> I don't understand.

> CARLOS
> Look into the Coronel; otherwise, there
> is nothing to do.

                                              CUT TO:

145 EXT. SERENITY OAKS - DAY   145

A peaceful wooded campus with a unobtrusive sign reading,
"Serenity Oaks Treatment Facility."

There are sayings on the walls: "Easy Does It;" "Let Go and
Let God;" "Turn it over;" "One Day at a Time..." "H.A.L.T. --
Hungry? Angry? Lonely? Tired?"

Caroline, wearing a thick, woolly sweater, and the other
PATIENTS sit around on beat-up couches and chairs in a loose
circle. It's a mixed BUNCH: trucker meth-head, rocker dope-
fiend, yuppie crack-head, fat, thin, rich, middle-class, and
all white. Caroline is the youngest.

MARTY, 40's, an overweight alcoholic, finishes his "share."

>   MARTY
>   ... So it was my birthday and my ex-wife
>   was getting remarried and I was in some
>   church basement telling a bunch of
>   strangers how it was a good day because I
>   didn't have to eat out of a dumpster.
>   That was enough to send me out on big
>   one.
>   (beat)
>   I've been thinking a lot about the first
>   step: that I came to believe I was
>   powerless over alcohol and that my life
>   had become unmanageable.
>   (beat)
>   See my disease tells me I don't have a
>   disease. That I'm fine. That it's my
>   birthday and I can have one little drink,
>   then one little line, then one little
>   Valium, then two more fat lines, then two
>   more 10 mil Valium... Six months later I
>   wake up in a sober living house in
>   Philly. And I'm from Dallas, people.
>   (beat)
>   It's a disease -- an allergy of the body
>   and an obsession of the mind. I know that
>   now. So my name's Marty and today I'm a
>   grateful recovering alcoholic who didn't
>   eat out of a dumpster. Thanks.

And Marty looks to Caroline who didn't relate to one word he
said.

>   CAROLINE
>   (slowly, very nervous)
>   Hi. I'm Caroline. I'm not sure I'm an
>   alcoholic.
>   (beat)
>   I mean I don't really like to drink.
>   (MORE)

(CONTINUED)

146 CONTINUED: 146

                          CAROLINE (cont'd)
                For someone my age it's so much easier to
                get drugs than beer. I don't know, this
                is really weird and I'm really nervous...

People in the room nod encouragingly.

                          CAROLINE (cont'd)
                I guess I'm angry. I mean I think I'm
                really angry about a lot of stuff, but I
                don't know what exactly.

She blushes, and stares out the window.

                                                        CUT TO:

147 INT. AYALA LIVING ROOM - AFTERNOON   147

Helena follows an ART APPRAISER through her formal living
room as he inspects paintings and makes notations. He is very
excited and moves quickly from one to the next.

                          ART APPRAISER
                Tamayo. Carrington. A simply wonderful
                collection of Mexican Modern. Give me
                three months. I know several collectors
                in South America, very discreet.

                          HELENA
                I don't have three months.

                          ART APPRAISER
                It takes time to find the proper
                collection.

                          HELENA
                How much will you give me in cash? Today.

The appraiser taps out some numbers on a calculator and shows
the figure to Helena.

                          HELENA (cont'd)
                You must be joking. That's a fraction of
                their value.

                          ART APPRAISER
                I'm sorry, but that is the figure I can
                get today.

Helena turns her back. She walks to a window and looks out,
then surveys the contents of her beautiful home.

                          HELENA
                        (snapping)
                Get out. Get out of my house.

                                                    (CONTINUED)

Helena turns and sees David in the doorway. She goes to him.

> HELENA (cont'd)
> It's all right. We're having a
> disagreement, that's all.

The art appraiser passes them on his way out.

148   INT. AYALA MASTER BEDROOM - NIGHT   148

Helena wakes up in the middle of the night with a start. Her
eyes are wide open. She has had a thought --

She climbs out of bed and quickly puts on a robe.

149   INT. UPSTAIRS HALLWAY - CONTINUOUS   149

Helena walks quickly and quietly down the hallway. She passes
David's room. She opens a door at the end of the hall --

150   INT. CARL'S PRIVATE STUDY - CONTINUOUS   150

Helena enters the room. She hits a desk lamp and we're in a
very comfortable and masculine upstairs study: bookshelves
holding hundreds of art books; comfortable chairs; MacIntosh
stereo; discreet flatscreen HD TV.

Helena stares at a painting on one of the bookshelves. It is
"Boy with a Hoop," a small portrait by Rafael Colonel.

She goes to it and looks from different angles. She reaches
out and jiggles the oil. Nothing happens. She looks behind
the painting at the backing.

She notices that one corner is not glued down. She picks up a
letter opener and pries the paper back. An envelope slips
out.

Inside the envelope: neat, thin strips of paper dense with
information in a miniscule type and a magnetic key card.

                                                          CUT TO:

151   OMITTED   151

152   OMITTED   152

153   OMITTED   153

A154 INT. HELICOPTER - DAY   A154

Robert and Sheridan ride in the back of the chopper. Each
looks out his own window.

                                                      (CONTINUED)

A154 CONTINUED: A154

     A newspaper on the seat between them shows a front page photo
     of General Salazar, exultant, and the headline reads in
     Spanish, "Salazar Named Chief of Anti-Narcotics Operations."

B154 EXT. MEXICO CITY - DAY   B154

     Establishing shot of a military helicopter landing on the
     roof of an office building in downtown Mexico City.

C154 INT. HEADQUARTERS, FEADS, - MEXICO CITY - DAY   C154

     Robert Wakefield and General Salazar stroll through the new
     headquarters where boxes are still being unpacked. Javier and
     Sheridan trail along behind them.

                         SALAZAR
                    I recruited the best men in Mexico for my
                    task force and put them through a
                    rigorous screening process. Not only
                    physical, but also psychological.

                         ROBERT
                    I'd like to bring you up to Washington,
                    walk you around our side of things, and
                    share some of the information we've been
                    able to develop on your cartels.

                         SALAZAR
                    That would be very helpful to me.
                         (beat)
                    Also, I received the offer from DEA and
                    the FBI to train some of my men at
                    Quantico. I think this will be extremely
                    useful, a good way for us to absorb some
                    of your methods.

D154 INT. SALAZAR'S I.N.C.D. OFFICE - DAY   D154

     The office hasn't been decorated yet.

                         SALAZAR
                    I've been too busy to completely settle
                    in.

     Salazar proffers a chair and they sit next to each other like
     Brezhnev and Nixon. PHOTOGRAPHERS begin SNAPPING pictures.
     After a few moments, Salazar waves them away, and they lower
     their cameras and leave.

                         ROBERT
                    You've been making very good progress
                    against the Tijuana cartel.

                                                   (CONTINUED)

> SALAZAR
> Yes, I am confident that Juan Obregon
> will be taken into custody before the end
> of the year. But, you must understand
> that it is very difficult because of
> corruption in the police force. We get a
> tip that he is one place, then we get
> there and he is already gone, having been
> warned by someone on our side.

> ROBERT
> Hopefully the exchange of training
> methods and information between our
> countries will help with this problem.

> SALAZAR
> Yes, I hope so as well.

> ROBERT
> Let me ask you a related question. We've
> talked about the supply side, but what
> about demand? What is your policy for
> treating addiction?

> SALAZAR
> Addicts treat themselves... they overdose
> and then there's one less to worry about.

Robert cannot respond.

CUT TO:

154   EXT. SERENITY OAKS - WALKWAY - DAY   154

Caroline ambles alone down a walkway at the treatment
facility.

She looks through the trees that surround the facility and
notices cars going by.

CUT TO:

155   INT. LOW-RENT HOTEL - DAY   155

Gordon and another DEA AGENT escort Ruiz up the stairs of a
large, older hotel.

> RUIZ
> This is ridiculous. Why is there no
> elevator?

(CONTINUED)

155 CONTINUED: 155

                         GORDON
                When the DEA gets into the narcotics
                business, then we'll stay at the Four
                Seasons.

They walk down a hotel hallway. Two more AGENTS stand outside
Room 407. Gordon opens the door and they enter.

156   INT. SUITE OF CHEAP HOTEL ROOMS - DAY   156

There are more AGENTS inside and old food and coffee
containers. Gordon gives Ruiz a tour. There are several
rooms. A bored Castro sits at a table staring at a Scrabble
board.

                         CASTRO
                Eddie, how you like your new home? I hope
                you hate it as much as I do.

Ruiz looks around with disgust. He's accustomed to finer
places. He goes to a window and looks out.

RUIZ'S POV: of the Federal Court building not far away.

                         RUIZ
                This is not what my lawyers negotiated.

Gordon pours himself a cup of coffee.

                         GORDON
                Fuck your lawyers. You aren't getting any
                cappuccino or Biscotti either.

157   INT. FEDERAL COURTHOUSE - DAY   157

A packed, tense courtroom listens to testimony from a
government witness, FRANK, 50's, very matter-of-fact and
truthful.

                         FRANK
                He first came to me in January. That
                would've been nineteen eighty-seven. He
                wanted to rent warehouse space along the
                harbor. I didn't ask too many questions;
                I'm a businessman also.

158   INT. FEDERAL COURTHOUSE - DAY   158

Another witness, MRS. BERRY, 40's, pedantic on the stand --

                         MRS. BERRY
                I told Mr. Ayala there were
                irregularities in his tax return.
                         (MORE)

                                              (CONTINUED)

                          MRS. BERRY (cont'd)
                    And I couldn't represent him unless we
                    could explain this...

159   INT. FEDERAL COURTHOUSE - DAY   159

        SHEILA, 38, a mousy secretary, is on the stand. Carlos sits
        at the defendant's table listening raptly. Gordon and Castro
        sit in the back watching Helena who pays close attention to
        the witness --

                          SHEILA
                    I was the company secretary from 1991 to
                    1994. I supposedly worked for all six
                    companies. But... they weren't... I mean,
                    it was just one empty office with a desk
                    and a telephone. We never sold anything
                    the whole time I was there. Sometimes
                    people came and got paid. I don't really
                    know what we did.

                          PROSECUTOR
                    Did Mr. Ayala say where the money came
                    from?

                          SHEILA
                    No, and I didn't ask.

                          PROSECUTOR
                    Where do you think it came from?

        Carl's lawyer, Adler, is on his feet --

                          KAUFMAN
                    This is speculation --

                          PROSECUTOR
                    I'll rephrase. Did you feel like you were
                    engaged in a legal enterprise?

        Sheila is reluctant to answer.

                          SHEILA
                    No, not really.

        Helena catches Carl's eye and they share a grim moment.

                                                            CUT TO:

160   OMITTED   160

161   OMITTED   161

162   OMITTED   162

163   OMITTED   163

164   INT. CARL'S UPSTAIRS STUDY - DAY   164

Helena sits at Carl's office desk. On the desk in front of
her are the lists she found and an encrypted cell phone.

Helena picks up the phone. Her hands are shaking. She is
crying as she dials. A voice on the other end answers.

                    FRANCISCO (V.O.)
          Who is this?

Helena gathers her courage, then...

                    HELENA
          A friend... of Carlos Ayala.

There is a long pause.

                    FRANCISCO (V.O.)
          Yes.

                    HELENA
          I'm on a special phone, may I speak
          freely?

                    FRANCISCO (V.O.)
          You may speak.

                    HELENA
          I have a job for you and I don't have
          much time.

165   EXT. BOTANICAL GARDEN - DAY   165

Helena watches David look at the wide variety of plants and
flowers. All around them a GROUP of 3rd graders, in identical
T-shirts, enjoy a field trip.

                    FRANCISCO (V.O.)
          I love this place. Don't turn around.

Behind her Francisco Flores takes a photo with an instant
camera.

                    FRANCISCO (cont'd)
          You were followed by the police, but they
          won't hear us over the children. I want
          to use a bomb.

                                        (CONTINUED)

                         HELENA
              You're kidding. Can't you shoot him or
              something?

                         FRANCISCO
              I don't really like guns. You shoot
              someone in the head three times and some
              doctor will keep them alive.

                         HELENA
              When will you do it?

                         FRANCISCO
              I don't know. Eduardo Ruiz is the only
              real witness against Carl. The security
              is very tight. There may not be a way.

                         HELENA
              There's always a way. If people get to
              the Pope or the President, you can get to
              him.

          Francisco laughs.

                         FRANCISCO
              Careful... You're sounding like your
              husband, Mrs. Ayala.

                                                        CUT TO:

165 OMITTED   166

167 OMITTED   167

A168 INT. JAVI'S APARTMENT - NIGHT   A168

     Anna sits in the living room, staring. She appears too upset
     to speak. The apartment is cleaner. There have been other
     changes. There's a new rug.

                         JAVIER
              What? What is it?

                         ANNA
              It's very hard for me to come and tell
              you this.

          Javier just watches her.

                         ANNA (cont'd)
              It's Manolo. He's going to do something
              stupid. I'm worried that he'll get
              himself killed.

                                                   (CONTINUED)

A168 CONTINUED: A168

He keeps watching.

> ANNA (cont'd)
> He's saying he's going to talk to the
> Americans. Become an informer. He says
> they pay a lot of money.

> JAVIER
> Why does he need money?

> ANNA
> He has debts. He has gambling debts. He
> owes a lot of money.

> JAVIER
> How much?

> ANNA
> Nine thousand dollars.

A long beat.

> JAVIER
> What is he planning on telling them?

> ANNA
> Well, you know, he's going to say about
> Madrigal... and Salazar.

Javier just looks at her.

                                                    CUT TO:

168   INT. ROBERT'S OFFICE IN WASHINGTON - DAY   168

Robert is on the telephone, listening. He is not happy.
Sheridan watches him.

> ROBERT
> (into phone)
> Nobody saw her leave?
> (beat)
> Yes... I understand.

He hangs up. He stands and reaches for his jacket.

> ROBERT (cont'd)
> I have to go. I have to go home.

169   INT. WAKEFIELD KITCHEN - NIGHT   169

Robert and Barbara sit at the kitchen table.

                                              (CONTINUED)

                              BARBARA
                    Should we bring the police into this?

                              ROBERT
                    No, not yet.

170 EXT. WEST END STREETS - DAY   170

     Robert drives through the streets in his Cadillac DeVille.

171 INT. DEVILLE - DAY   171

     Robert rides in glum silence. He looks at passersby who are
     almost all black and almost all stare back at the white man
     in his Cadillac.

     A group of young men stare threateningly as he rolls past.

     On the street, in the lee of a Brownstone staircase, a deal
     is going down.

A172 ROBERT AND SETH ABRAHMS - DAY   A172

     sit in a coffee shop.

                              SETH
                         (genuinely surprised)
                    She's not at that place you sent her?

                              ROBERT
                    She snuck away. And we haven't seen her.
                    She hasn't come home.

                              SETH
                    Oh, man --

                              ROBERT
                    She hasn't called you?

                              SETH
                    I tried to talk to her when she was up
                    there, but they wouldn't put me through.
                         (beat)
                    I'm surprised she hasn't called.

172 ANOTHER ANGLE ON ROBERT IN THE CAR - DAY   172

     He turns a corner and is suddenly in a drive-thru drug
     market. Dealers, HUSTLERS, run at the windows from both
     sides, signalling.

                                                        (CONTINUED)

172 CONTINUED: 172

                    HUSTLERS
          What you want? Rock? Rock? Hey, what you
          want?

A173 ROBERT AND SETH - DAY   A173

     in the coffee shop.

                    ROBERT
          Can you tell me anything? Do you have any
          ideas?

                    SETH
          I don't know what to say.

                    ROBERT
          I'm not the police. I don't care about
          experimentation. She's a kid. I'm worried
          to death.

                    SETH
          You won't say anything to my parents?

                    ROBERT
          I don't give a fuck about your parents --

                    SETH
          We sometimes went downtown to score.

                    ROBERT
          What?

                    SETH
          The West End. We buy it off the streets.
               (beat)
          I can stop, you know, and she can't. Two
          people, really similar, we can talk about
          anything, but for me it's like a weekend
          thing, then I get my shit together, and
          for her it's different --

                    ROBERT
          You don't know what the hell you're
          talking about. You're a cocky seventeen
          year-old and you don't have a clue what
          the stakes are. You don't know the value
          of the life you've yet to throw away. And
          neither does she.

173 ROBERT IN HIS CAR - DAY   173

     It is surrounded. Robert stares. A face presses up against
     the window.

                                        (CONTINUED)

>   FACE
>   (through the window)
>   What do you want?
>
>   ROBERT
>   (through the window)
>   What do you mean, what do I want?
>
>   FACE
>   Rock or dope, man?
>
>   ROBERT
>   I don't want anything.

174   ROBERT AND SETH   174

>   SETH
>   Hey man, I'm sorry. I'm just trying to
>   help.
>
>   ROBERT
>   You want to help? Stay the fuck away from
>   her.

A175 ROBERT IN HIS CAR   A175

>   ROBERT (cont'd)
>   I'm looking for my daughter.

The dealer looks at him with disgust, turns his back, and waves everyone else away.

Robert slams his fist against the steering wheel. He slams it again and again. He stops and pulls away, just as

AT THE INTERSECTION

behind Robert's car, Caroline crosses the street toward Sketch's house.

175   INT. SKETCH'S BEDROOM - DAY   175

A single candle lights the room. Caroline is underneath Sketch the drug dealer. He is pounding away. As she clutches his back and holds on, her expression is both surprised and druggy, and SOUNDS escape her mouth that she wouldn't believe she could make.

There's a KNOCK on the door. Sketch continues his business. The KNOCKING is more insistent. Finally, he stops and gets up and goes to the door. Caroline lies back. She's in a bed with black sheets in a room with nothing else in it but a dresser and some duffle bags.

                                                    (CONTINUED)

Sketch opens the door --

> SKETCH
> What the fuck do you want?

SOMEBODY outside says something. Sketch walks over to a
duffle bag and extracts some product. Caroline's eyes are
glued to it as Sketch hands it through the door. Sketch sees
her staring at the drugs.

He comes back to bed.

> SKETCH (CONT'D)
> You want some of that?

Caroline nods.

> SKETCH (cont'd)
> What you gonna do to get some of that?

> CAROLINE
> Please --

> SKETCH
> What you gonna do?

She turns her back to him, pouting. He laughs.

> SKETCH (CONT'D)
> Maybe a taste.

He reaches over beside the bed where there is a small tray.
On the tray is a rig, spoon, several powders, and an eye
dropper. He pulls the candle over and rapidly fixes a
speedball. He pulls the fluid into the neck of the syringe
and holds it up the light. It has Caroline transfixed.

> SKETCH (cont'd)
> Feed this to you like a little bird.

He squirts the tiniest amount of fluid into the air. It arcs
in the candlelight.

> CAROLINE
> Don't --

> SKETCH
> You want this?

She nods.

(CONTINUED)

                              SKETCH (cont'd)
                    This is the Express train. Baby turnin'
                    pro and getting down in a big, big hole.

Her concentration is entirely, hypnotically focused on the
syringe.

Sketch moves the syringe toward her lips.

                              SKETCH (cont'd)
                    Kiss it. Kiss your new mommy hello.

Caroline moves her mouth toward the side of the syringe, her
lips part.

Sketch pulls the sheet back, exposing her legs. He grips one
powerful hand around her ankle and squeezes... Veins stand
out on her foot.

He slides the needle into the largest vein and slowly
depresses the plunger.

Caroline watches, then her head tilts back, then forward, she
GROANS sexually and slumps against the pillows, her eyes half-
open, her lips twitching.

Sketch puts the rig back on the tray, then admires Caroline's
beauty for a second before starting to fuck her again.

                                                         CUT TO:

176   EXT. HOTEL - DAY   176

      Gordon and Castro and two other AGENTS escort Ruiz out of the
      hotel and usher him into a waiting cruiser.

      They pull out in a caravan and move through the streets
      toward the courthouse.

177   EXT. COURTHOUSE PARKING LOT - DAY   177

      The cruiser pulls into a fenced and gated parking lot.

      Gordon, Castro and Ruiz, walking with a limp, cross to the
      building entrance.

      As they push inside, Francisco Flores, in a conservative grey
      suit passes them going outside.

      The parking lot is empty of people. The guards at the gate
      talk about something distracting.

                                                      (CONTINUED)

Francisco passes by the cruiser and drops his keys. Kneeling
down he extracts a small, powerful, magnetized bomb from his
jacket. He attaches it to the underside of the vehicle,
stands and walks toward the guard gate.

178   INT. COURTROOM - DAY   178

The court is filled to capacity. Helena and Metzger watch
from the gallery.

The JUDGE bangs his gavel. Adler is on his feet.

                    ADLER
          Your honor, it has come to our attention
          that your honor, while in private
          practice, previously represented the town
          of Seal Beach in their stop-work suit
          against the Police Department of Seal
          Beach. We believe this disqualifies you
          from hearing this case and we therefore
          move for a temporary suspension while
          this is investigated.

The judge is surprised to hear this.

                    JUDGE
          Mr. Adler, this is a most unusual motion.

                    ADLER
          Nonetheless, your honor, we feel that our
          client deserves every fairness afforded
          under the law.

                    JUDGE
          If this is in any way designed to delay
          the testimony of Eduardo Ruiz...

The judge considers.

                    JUDGE (CONT'D)
          We'll recess until 9:00 am Monday
          morning. And I'll see counsel in
          chambers.

He slams the gavel down again.

179   EXT. COURTHOUSE - DAY   179

Gordon, Castro, other AGENTS and Ruiz come down the rear
steps of the courthouse and walk across the street toward the
parking lot.

                                                  (CONTINUED)

                    CASTRO
          Remember when we sat on that mob guy,
          that chef, for like six months?

                    GORDON
          Oh, man, I've never eaten so good in my
          life.
               (to Ruiz)
          Why don't you develop a useful skill?

                    CASTRO
          Yeah, like turning into a beautiful
          woman.

They reach the car.

                    RUIZ
          Would you mind if today we walked? It's
          one block. I could use the fresh air.

180   OMITTED   180

181   INT. FRANCISCO'S CAR - CONTINUOUS   181

Across the street, Francisco, encrypted cell phone to his
ear, watches from his own car as Gordon, Castro, and Ruiz
stand by their car without getting in, then walk away from
the car.

                    FRANCISCO
               (into phone)
          They're not getting into the car. What
          are they doing? They're walking right at
          me.

The men start across the street toward Francisco.

182   INT. HELENA'S CAR - DAY   182

Helena drives her car through downtown San Diego.

                    HELENA
               (into phone)
          You've got a gun. Get out of the car and
          shoot him in the head.

183   INT. FRANCISCO'S CAR - DAY   183

Francisco watches Ruiz and the agents walk up the street
toward him.

                                            (CONTINUED)

183 CONTINUED: 183

                         FRANCISCO
                        (into phone)
                  They're going to walk right past me.

                         HELENA (V.O.)
                  What are you? A mouse? Get out of the car
                  and do it. This is your chance.

       Francisco watches the three men walk past his car. He makes a
       decision and opens his door.

184 EXT. STREET - DAY   184

       Francisco steps from the car and mingles in with OTHER PEOPLE
       walking along the sidewalk. He follows them for few yards,
       picking his moment.

       He closes the distance to Gordon, Castro and Ruiz, pulling a
       pistol from inside his jacket. He takes careful aim from
       twelve feet away and is about to shoot Ruiz when a bullet
       hole appears in his chest. He staggers, trying to squeeze the
       trigger,

       Francisco fires the gun once, wildly --

       A TOURIST SCREAMS --

       Gordon and Castro and Ruiz turn --

       Francisco is looking down at the widening red splotch in the
       center of his shirt, uncertain of what has happened --

       Gordon shoves Ruiz down into a doorway and fires three quick
       shots --

       Francisco spins around and drops on his face in the street.

       Citizens run in all directions fearing a psychopath with an
       NRA card coming off a bad week of day-trading --

       Gordon and Castro with Ruiz beneath them scan the streets.

                         CASTRO
                  Stay here. I'll get the car.

       Castro runs down the street for the court parking lot. Other
       AGENTS are running toward Gordon and Ruiz.

185 INT. OFFICE BUILDING WINDOW - CONTINUOUS   185

       The STRANGE MAN who threatened Helena's children packs a high-
       caliber rifle and scope into a briefcase.

                                                        (CONTINUED)

185 CONTINUED: 185

He snaps the case shut and quickly exits the room. We notice
a man on the floor with a bullet hole in his head next to the
open door.

186 EXT. STREET - CONTINUOUS   186

Agents surround Ruiz.

Gordon walks to the body of Francisco lying face down in the
gutter. He turns him over with his shoe and sees his face.

                        GORDON
                   (to the other agents)
               I saw this guy at the courthouse.
                   (beat)
               The car --

Gordon takes off running, yelling for Castro.

187 EXT. COURT PARKING LOT - DAY   187

Castro has reached the car and gets in.

Gordon appears at the gate of the lot --

                        GORDON
                   (yelling)
               No --

188 INT. CRUISER - DAY   188

Castro turns the ignition exactly at the moment he sees
Gordon yelling and waving his arms --

189 EXT. COURT PARKING LOT - DAY   189

The cruiser EXPLODES.

Gordon hits the pavement. Parts of the car begin raining down
around him.

                                                         CUT TO:

190 OMITTED   190

A191 INT. SIDEWALK CAFE - SAN DIEGO - DAY   A191

A fire truck and paramedic unit WHIZZES by. Manolo sits at an
outdoor cafe table, waiting. He can't help looking around at
the attractive people, but he's also nervous.

                                                    (CONTINUED)

Suddenly two MEN, recognizable as Salazar's OFFICERS from the
desert drug bust, sitting at a nearby table, rise and move to
Manolo's table.

> MAN #1
> Manolo, how are you?

They take seats uncomfortably close to Manolo.

> MAN #2
> Manolo, have we interrupted? You're
> looking around like you're expecting
> someone.

> MANOLO
> No. I'm looking for the waiter. I want to
> order.

> MAN #1
> What are you gonna have?

> MANOLO
> A steak.

> MAN #1
> Well, if you like steak, we know a much
> better place. We'll take you there.

> MANOLO
> That's okay, really.

They each take Manolo by an arm.

> MAN #2
> Manolo, we should really be going now,
> before it gets too crowded.

A191 INT. SUV - DAY   B191

We're looking through the windshield as we approach the
Mexican border. As the car slows, we pan to follow the border
official as he looks in briefly and waves us through. We
continue the pan to reveal Manolo in the backseat sitting
beside Man #2.

191 INT. SUV - DAY   C191

We're in the desert. There's nothing in any direction. Javi
is implacable. Manolo understands what is happening.

                                                      (CONTINUED)

                              MANOLO
                    I was going to feed them wrong
                    information. Feed them lies to ... it was
                    for...

The men say nothing. After a beat --

                              MANOLO (CONT'D)
                    Don't tell Anna I died like this. Tell
                    her it was something else. Tell her it
                    was official business. Tell her that I
                    died doing something honorable. Please,
                    tell her that for me...

EXT. DESERT - DAY

Javi and Manolo stand next to two freshly dug graves.

                              MAN #1
                    Turn around.

Javi hesitates before turning. We're on Javi as we hear the
GUNSHOT. Javi doesn't flinch. Manolo's body falls into the
grave.

Javi stands there, waiting.

                              MAN #1 (CONT'D)
                    You got anything you want to say?

Javi shakes his head. Finally, another GUNSHOT. After a beat,
a hand reaches out of Javi's shoulder.

                              MAN #1 (CONT'D)
                    Sorry about that... we had to be sure.

They walk back to the SUV.

                              SOMEBODY ELSE
                    Are you sure you don't have anything to
                    tell us?

Javi says nothing, doesn't even acknowledge them. We hear a
GUNSHOT.

                                                              CUT TO:

191 INT. AYALA HOME - DAY   191

     Arnie Metzger is in Helena's living room. The stereo is
     loudly playing MOZART.

                                                          (CONTINUED)

                    ARNIE
          That was a stupid thing you did.
          Incredibly stupid.

                    HELENA
          I tried, Arnie. And, I will continue to
          try.

                    ARNIE
          Have you gone crazy? You are not Carl.
          You aren't as good as Carl.
                    (beat)
          They are moving the trial to a high
          security location. The press has gone
          berserk. The jury will be influenced.
          Stay out of things. Let us try to win the
          case.

                    HELENA
          That is going to be rather difficult when
          all the evidence is against us.

Helena steps closer to Arnie, close enough that her breasts
are almost touching his chest.

                    ARNIE
          Helena, please. This is out of your
          hands.

                    HELENA
                    (softly)
          I know I made things worse. I know that
          and I'm sorry, but Arnie I need something
          from you. Something only you can help me
          with.

Helena looks searchingly into his eyes.

                    ARNIE
          Helena --

                    HELENA
          I need an introduction to the Obregon
          Brothers.

                    ARNIE
          I can't do that.

Helena leans closer to him.

(CONTINUED)

                    HELENA
          I've figured out what Carl was up to and
          I need your help. Will you help me?

                                                    CUT TO:

192 EXT. LABORATORY RESEARCH FACILITIES - DAY   192

     An establishing shot of a hi-tech company within shooting
     distance of the Salk Institute.

193 INT. LAB FACILITY - DAY   193

     This is a professional chemical lab that can be rented by the
     month. Long tables of lab and computer equipment. Nobody has
     been here in a while. There are toys - plastic dolls,
     frisbees, hula hoops - on many of the tables.

     Helena lets herself into the room. She scans ledgers. She
     looks over the equipment.

     She picks up a twelve-inch high plastic Spastic Jack action
     figure and a can labeled "solvent" and hurries from the lab.

                                                    CUT TO:

194 EXT. WEST END - CINCINNATI - NIGHT   194

     Robert drives through the streets, searching for Caroline. He
     doesn't find her.

195 INT. WAKEFIELD HOUSE - NIGHT   195

     Barbara is waiting in the living room. Robert enters. He
     shakes his head then stands silently for a beat.

                    ROBERT
          About the other night, I'm sorry.

                    BARBARA
          Me, too.

                    ROBERT
          God, I don't get it. Are we supposed to
          say to ourselves, be prepared to lose
          her, be prepared to lose our child?
               (beat)
          Why does this happen to someone? How does
          it happen?

                    BARBARA
          I don't know.

196   INT. CAROLINE'S BEDROOM - NIGHT   196

Robert is standing in the middle of her room. He's not sure
what he's looking for. Everywhere he looks: her personal
things, beloved objects from more innocent times, pictures.

Within moments a legitimate desire to connect with his
daughter has escalated into a search for clues. He opens her
drawers, dumps little boxes, pulls things off of shelves.

He becomes increasingly unhinged, flinging things around her
room. He tosses a stack of magazines. A fashion magazine,
airborne, discharges some contents: a lighter, a plastic tube
and a piece of folded aluminum foil fluttering to the ground.

Robert stares at the foil on the carpet. It's charred on the
outside. He picks it up. And unfolds it. There's a dried
milky white substance.

He picks up the tube and lighter and stares at them. Then,
somewhat tentatively, he puts the tube in his mouth. He holds
the lighter under the foil, then heats the milky substance
which turns translucent and disappears in a cloud of smoke.
Robert sucks all of it in.

He waits a long time then exhales. His eyes shut. The tube
drops from his mouth. He staggers and, overwhelmed by the
sensations, sits on the bed. The lighter and foil fall from
his hand.

A moment later he opens his eyes and doesn't seem to know
where he is. He looks at the room, confused. He stumbles to
the door and shuts it firmly behind him.

                                                    CUT TO:

197   INT. MANOLO'S HOUSE - DAY   A197

Anna is weeping. Javier sits next to her. He puts his arm
around her and she leans her head against his shoulder.

197   INT. JAVIER'S SUV - DAY   B197

Javi drives through the streets of Tijuana. He brakes for a
stop sign and watches, trance-like, the pedestrians crossing
in front of him. As the intersection clears he remains still.

A HONK from behind brings him back and he pulls forward
passing Helena Ayala who crosses going the opposite
direction. We stay with her.

                                                    CUT TO:

197   EXT. TIJUANA - DAY   197

     Helena walks down a nightlife street that is tawdry and stale
     in the midday sun.

198   OMITTED   198

199   INT. CLUB PLATINUM - DAY   199

     A shrewd Obregon Lieutenant, JUAN MARQUEZ, 40, sits at a
     table opposite Helena. The Strange Man who both threatened
     Helena's child and executed Francisco sits in another chair.

                         MARQUEZ
               Mrs. Ayala. Thank you for coming. I am
               Juan Marquez, I work for Mr. Obregon. I
               believe you know my associate,
               "Tigrillo," the Little Tiger.

     Helena nods to Tigrillo --

                         HELENA
               Yes, he threatened to kill my five year-
               old son.
                    (beat)
               I was under the impression I would be
               meeting Juan Obregon.

                         MARQUEZ
               No, that is not possible. And thank you
               for coming down here, though I suspect
               it's been a pointless journey.

                         HELENA
               Why do you say that, Mr. Marquez?

                         MARQUEZ
               I hear these stories. Your husband in
               jail. His business in chaos. Various
               people fighting over the scraps.

                         HELENA
               My husband is the victim of an informer
               in your organization, not ours.

                         MARQUEZ
               That is not true, Mrs. Ayala. Your route
               is compromised. Perhaps it is time for me
               to deal with other distributors in
               California.

                         HELENA
               I don't think you're going to do that.

                                                    (CONTINUED)

> MARQUEZ
> You don't? Listen to this woman in a
> man's world, a very violent world.

> HELENA
> There are plenty of other suppliers in
> Mexico.

> MARQUEZ
> But not in whose interest it is to help
> you out of debt.

Helena reaches into her bag and pulls out the Spastic Jack
action figure. She puts it on the desk.

> HELENA
> My husband had been working on something
> he called, *The Project for the Children.*
> Are you aware of this?

> MARQUEZ
> I don't know. Perhaps I remember
> something.

> HELENA
> We have the ability to change the color,
> odor, and physical property of cocaine.

> MARQUEZ
> You want to smuggle narcotics in Mr.
> Espastico Jacobo. That's nothing new.

> HELENA
> Not *in*...

Juan Marquez is confused.

> HELENA (cont'd)
> This doll *is* cocaine.

Juan picks up Spastic Jack and looks at him. He bangs it on
the desk.

> HELENA (cont'd)
> Every part, from his ears to his
> accessory belt, is high-impact, pressure-
> molded cocaine. Odorless. Undetectable by
> dogs. Undetectable by anyone.

> MARQUEZ
> I don't believe you.

She takes out the "solvent" and puts it on his desk.

(CONTINUED)

                          HELENA
                    Get a bowl.

200   INT. CLUB PLATINUM - OFFICE - LATER   200

      Spastic Jack is slowly dissolving in a bowl of solvent. Only
      his shoulders, head, and ridiculous ears remain above the
      quicksand of milky glop.

      Helena holds a mirror under the desk lamp. She is drying the
      paste. She puts the mirror on the desk. A white substance has
      coagulated there.

                          HELENA
                    Try it.

      Juan takes out a razor blade and chops the dried substance
      into two white powder lines. He hands a silver straw to
      Helena.

                          MARQUEZ
                    You first.

                          HELENA
                    I'm six months pregnant. I won't do it.

                          MARQUEZ
                    Fine, then we don't have deal.

                          HELENA
                    Fine, then we don't have a deal.

      She stands. He watches her a beat, then smiles.

                          MARQUEZ
                    Okay, okay.

      He leans down and quickly snorts a line. After a beat.

                          Marquez (cont'd)
                    That's good coke.

                          HELENA
                    It should be... It's yours.
                        (beat)
                    I want our debt forgiven. I want to be
                    the exclusive distributor of Obregon
                    Brothers Cocaine for the United States.
                    And I want the principle witness against
                    my husband, Eduardo Ruiz, killed.

                                                        (CONTINUED)

                         MARQUEZ
              Perhaps... Perhaps... I'm afraid I must
              first ask you to pass a test. I asked the
              same of your husband and he succeeded
              with flying colors.

Helena waits. Juan Marquez reaches in his desk and pulls out
a quarter kilo of cocaine. He pushes it across the desk.

                         MARQUEZ (cont'd)
              Take this back with you. Deliver it
              safely to Tigrillo in San Diego and we
              have a deal.

                         HELENA
              That's crazy. My husband is on trial for
              smuggling.

                         MARQUEZ
              Exactly, and this is how I know I'm not
              getting into business with the U.S.
              Government.

She puts the quarter key in her bag and stands.

                         HELENA
              You will help me with my other problem.

                         MARQUEZ
              Deliver that safely to Tigrillo in San
              Diego. And we have a deal.

Tigrillo escorts her out of the room.

201   INT. CLUB PLATINUM - DAY   201

Helena follows Tigrillo. As they pass the restrooms she
signals that she has to stop.

202   INT. CLUB PLATINUM - LADIES' ROOM - DAY   202

Helena goes into a stall. She extracts the cocaine from her
handbag.

She looks at it, trying to figure out where it goes. She
hikes up her skirt.

                                                          CUT TO:

203   OMITTED   203

204   OMITTED   204

205	OMITTED	205
206	OMITTED	206
207	OMITTED	207
208	OMITTED	208
209	OMITTED	209
210	INT. HOTEL ROOM - DAY	210

Javier is hooked up to a polygraph machine watched closely by a POLYGRAPH OPERATOR. Hughes and Johnson watch as Javi talks into a tape recorder on the table.

                    JAVIER
          ... And I have the electronic serial
          numbers for their cellular phones. They
          change them every twenty-four hours but I
          have a contact at MexTel who can get me
          the new ESNs within twelve.

Javi finishes talking and sits back. Agent Hughes shuts off the tape recorder and looks at the polygraph operator who nods approval. Hughes and Johnson exchange a look. They are dumbstruck.

                    HUGHES
          That's good shit.

                    JAVIER
          Now that you have what you want, let's
          talk about how I get what I want.

                    JOHNSON
          Oh, don't worry, Javier, you're not gonna
          have any problems there.

                    HUGHES
          I want to take a minute and talk about
          what type of precautions you're taking to
          protect yourself. When Salazar and
          Madrigal go down, they might send someone
          to see you.

                    JAVIER
          You worry about getting me the things
          that I want. I'll worry about myself.

There's a beat. Javier seems discomfited. The two agents notice this and exchange looks.

                                        (CONTINUED)

210 CONTINUED: 210

>   JOHNSON
>   You should feel good about this.

>   JAVIER
>   I feel like a traitor.

CUT TO:

211 OMITTED 211

212 OMITTED 212

213 EXT. BORDER CROSSING AUTOMOBILE CHECKPOINT - DAY 213

Javi goes into Mexico. Pan over to Helena's Mercedes.

214 INT. HELENA'S CAR - DAY 214

She inches the car forward towards the officer who selects
vehicles for inspection. The car ahead of her passes through
and speeds away. The OFFICER flags Helena and directs her
into the search facility.

215 EXT. CUSTOMS SEARCH BAY - DAY 215

Helena pulls into a search bay.

A CUSTOMS OFFICER watches Helena lower her window.

>   CUSTOMS OFFICER
>   Please step from the car, Ma'am.

>   HELENA
>   I'm in a hurry --

>   CUSTOMS OFFICER
>   Step from the car, Ma'am. This won't take
>   long from your day.

Helena gets out of her car.

216 INT. OBSERVATION ROOM - CUSTOMS CHECKPOINT - DAY 216

There is a bank of video monitors showing the scenes all over
the facility.

ON THE MONITOR: Helena's car is on a lift three feet off the
ground. Officers pour over the inside and undercarriage of
the Mercedes.

Nearby, A GERMAN SHEPHERD sniffs at the items that have been
removed from the car: bags, spare tire, cd boxes.

217 EXT. CUSTOMS SEARCH BAY - DAY

      Customs OFFICERS approach Helena --

                        OFFICER
            Ma'am, we have to ask you to come with
            us.

      She follows them toward the Customs building.

218 INT. STRIP SEARCH ROOM - DAY   218

      A FEMALE CUSTOMS INSPECTOR accompanied by a female
      SUPERVISORY INSPECTOR leads Helena into a sterile room where
      there is no place to hide anything.

                        CUSTOMS MATRON
            Ma'am, we have reason to believe you may
            have illegal drugs hidden beneath your
            clothing. I need to conduct a pat down
            search. Supervisory Inspector Haig will
            witness the search.

                        HELENA
            You've got to be kidding me. I'm
            pregnant. What if I refuse?

                        CUSTOMS MATRON
            This pamphlet explains the law and your
            rights under it. You're welcome to read
            it first. It says we have the authority
            to conduct this search. Would you like to
            read it first or shall we proceed?

A219 EXT. FUNERAL SERVICE - DAY   A219

      Hundreds of DEA AGENTS, spouses, others stand around a grave
      in a leafy cemetery in working class San Diego.

B219 EXT. CEMETERY - DAY   B219

      The funeral is over and people are filing back to the cars.
      Gordon walks away from the service when he is approached by a
      mourning LUCINDA CASTRO, the mother of the deceased.

                        MRS. CASTRO
            Montel... Oh, Montel.

      Gordon hugs her.

                        MRS. CASTRO (cont'd)
            You know how much he cared about you. You
            do, don't you?

                                                    (CONTINUED)

                         GORDON
          Yes.

                         MRS. CASTRO
          I know if he could have it back somehow,
          he wouldn't do it differently or have it
          any other way. He wouldn't. He loved his
          job.

Another AGENT hustles toward him from the other direction,
the direction of the cars.

                         AGENT
          Excuse me, Agent Gordon. Mrs. Castro.
               (to Gordon)
          Helena Ayala left Club Platinum in
          Tijuana. The Obregon Brothers' place.
          They stopped her at the border but she
          was clean. She's in San Diego now.

Gordon runs for his car.

                                                    CUT TO:

19   INT. ARNIE METZGER'S OFFICE - DAY   219

Arnie sits in his office, spacing out, admiring his view when
an ASSISTANT shows Helena in. As soon as the door shuts --

                         HELENA
          Did you get it?

                         ARNIE
          What are you thinking, calling me at home
          with a message like that? You've
          compromised me and our relationship --

Helena sits confidently on his couch.

                         HELENA
               (making fun of Arnie)
          The place is swept twice a day. I learned
          that down in Miami in '85...
               (hard)
          Arnie. I'm the housewife. I belong to the
          most exclusive country club in La Jolla
          that accepts Latinos. Until recently, I
          believed my husband imported hydroponic
          strawberries, which I donated at the
          school fair.

Arnie reaches into a desk drawer and pulls out a quarter-kilo
baggy identical to the one Juan Obregon gave her in Tijuana.

                                              (CONTINUED)

                              HELENA (CONT'D)
                    It's the same stuff? From the rainy day
                    stash?

                              ARNIE
                    It's the same. What happened to what they
                    gave you?

          Helena puts the bag in her purse.

                              HELENA
                    I'm desperate, but I'm not stupid. I
                    flushed it in the bathroom of their
                    godawful nightclub.

                                                            CUT TO:

220 OMITTED   220

A221 INT. ROBERT AND BARBARA'S BEDROOM - EARLY MORNING   A221

          Robert sleeps in his clothes on top of the covers. Barbara is
          asleep beside him. The phone rings. Robert answers. Barbara
          watches.

                              ROBERT
                    Hello.

                              SHERIDAN (V.O.)
                    I'm sorry... Did I wake you?

          Robert looks at Barbara and shakes his head. She gets up.

                              ROBERT
                    No, it's all right.

          There's a beat.

                              SHERIDAN (V.O.)
                    Salazar's been taken down. He was working
                    for Porfirio Madrigal.

                              ROBERT
                    What? I thought Madrigal was dead. I
                    thought it was verified.

                              SHERIDAN (V.O.)
                    Apparently not. Look, it's a shit storm
                    here right now. When are you coming back?
                         (beat)
                    I don't know what to tell people any
                    more.

                                                    (CONTINUED)

                              ROBERT
              I'll get there as soon as I can.

                              SHERIDAN (V.O.)
              If we're moving the press conference, we
              need to do it now.
                    (beat)
              Are you all right?

                              BARBARA WAKEFIELD (V.O.)
              Robert.

The tone in Barbara's voice causes him to look up. She holds
an empty jewelry box.

                              ROBERT
                    (to Sheridan)
              I have to call you back.

B221   INT. DINING ROOM - EARLY MORNING   B221

The drawers and cabinets are open. Barbara and Robert assess
what is missing.

                              BARBARA
              The silver wedding cup.

C221   INT. LIVING ROOM - EARLY MORNING   C221

Robert looks at their home entertainment center. Barbara
enters this room.

                              BARBARA
              My Leica's gone.

                              ROBERT
              So's the video camera.

                              BARBARA
              At least she's alive.

Robert turns for the door.

                              BARBARA (cont'd)
              Where are you going?

                              ROBERT
              She'll be at a pawn shop in an hour. Ten
              minutes after that she'll be at her
              dealer's. If I find him, maybe I find
              her.

D221 INT. CLASSROOM - CINCINNATI COUNTRY DAY - DAY   D221

The bored children of privilege, wearing their blazers or
uniform grey skirts, stare at a TEACHER behind a desk.

The door opens and Robert enters. He finds Seth Abrahms in
the back of the class and walks straight to him. Robert grabs
a fistful of shirt and tie.

                    SETH
          Hey man, what are you doing?

                    TEACHER (O.S.)
          Excuse me? Excuse me?

Robert yanks Seth out of his seat. The teacher is
approaching.

                    ROBERT
          Seth has to be excused. He's going on a
          field trip.

221 INT. THE FUN ZONE - DAY   221

Helena watches David play a video game. They have finished
their lunch, a mess of pizza rinds.

                    HELENA
          Come on. Time to go.

The CLOWN tries to catch their attention with some mime, but
they ignore him.

222 EXT. THE FUN ZONE - DAY   222

Helena and David are pushing out the door. The man walking
the other way past them is Tigrillo from the Tijuana cartel.
As they pass --

                    HELENA
               (under her breath)
          Women's room, stall two.
               (loud)
          Should we stop for ice-cream?

                    DAVID
          Yeah!

Tigrillo disappears into the restaurant.

                                                  (CONTINUED)

As Helena pulls out of the Fun Zone parking lot, an unmarked
DEA cruiser falls in behind her.

                                                    CUT TO:

A223   INT. ROBERT'S CAR - DAY   A223

Robert and Seth are parked across the street from Sketch's
building. They watch people, mostly white people, get what
they need.

                    SETH
          I don't know, maybe we missed her.

                    ROBERT
          I can't believe you used to bring my
          daughter here, to this place.

                    SETH
          Hey man, back the fuck up. *To this place.*
          What's that shit? Right now, all over
          this country, a hundred thousand white
          people from the suburbs are driving
          around downtown asking every black person
          they see, *You got any drugs? You know
          where I can get drugs?* What kind of
          effect you think this has on the psyche
          of a black person, on their
          possibilities? If you sent a hundred
          thousand black people into *your*
          neighborhood, Indian Hills, and they
          asked every white person they saw, *hey,
          you got any drugs?*, within a day, your
          friends and their kids would be selling.
          It's market forces, man. The product's
          marked up three hundred percent. You can
          go out on the street and make five
          hundred bucks in two hours and then do
          whatever you want for the rest of the
          day. You think white people would still
          be going to law school?

There's a beat.

                    ROBERT
          You're starting to piss me off. Get out
          of the car.

Robert and Seth get our of the car and walk across the
street.

Robert and Seth stand in the dim, dingy hallway. A JUNKIE leaves.

                    SETH
          You're gonna get me killed.

Robert shoves Seth toward the door. Seth knocks. The door opens a crack and Sketch's face appears.

                    SKETCH
          What do you want?

Robert moves around Seth.

                    ROBERT
          I'm looking for my daughter, Caroline.
          She comes here.

                    SKETCH
          This is a business. Get the fuck outta
          here.

                    ROBERT
          I need to find my daughter. I'll pay you.

Sketch pulls a gun and shoves it against Robert's cheek.

                    SKETCH
          Who the fuck do you think you are? Where
          the fuck do you think you are? Why the
          fuck do you think I shouldn't just put
          you in a dumpster?

                    ROBERT
          I have money --

                    SKETCH
          I got money.

                    ROBERT
          I'll pay you a thousand dollars. I have
          it in my wallet.

                    SKETCH
          I want your money, I'll take your money.

                    ROBERT
          Just tell me where she is.

                                              (CONTINUED)

B223 CONTINUED: B223

        Sketch pushes Robert back into the hall. Sketch sees Seth
        lurking there.

                          SKETCH
                      (to Seth)
                  Don't do that shit again.

        Sketch slams the door in their face.

                          SETH
                  Great. What a good idea.

C223 EXT. STREET - DAY   C223

        Seth and Robert walk to the car.

                          SETH
                  Man, I'm telling you. Don't do this
                  vigilante thing. Either the cops find her
                  or she'll call you. I promise.

        Robert looks at him, carefully.

                                                          CUT TO:

D223 EXT. MANOLO'S HOUSE - DAY   D223

        Javier KNOCKS on the front door. There is no answer. The
        shades are drawn. The house is darkened.

                          JAVIER
                      (calling out)
                  Anna. Anna, please. Let me in.

        He KNOCKS again.

                          JAVIER (cont'd)
                  Come on. You can't stay locked in your
                  house all day.

        Finally, the door cracks open. Anna has clearly not been out
        of the house since the last time we saw her.

E223 INT. MANOLO'S HOUSE - DAY   E223

        Javier sits opposite Anna.

                          JAVIER
                  I know this is a tragedy, but you have to
                  realize that good has come out of it.

        She looks at him.

                                                      (CONTINUED)

                         JAVIER (cont'd)
                    If Manolo hadn't gone and told them what
                    he did then Salazar and Madrigal would
                    never have been brought to justice. He
                    did a great thing for Tijuana. He did a
                    great thing for Mexico.

                         ANNA
                    I want to believe you. I really do.

                         JAVIER
                    You will believe me, because it's true.

223 EXT. SKETCH'S APARTMENT - DAY   223

     Seth walks up the steps and into the building. A beat later
     he reappears and continues down the street.

     Robert emerges from across the street and follows at a
     guarded distance.

224 EXT. STREETS - DAY   224

     Seth walks along the seedy neighborhood street. He approaches
     the Villa Elaine. He turns up the steps and disappears
     inside.

     Robert follows him.

225 INT. VILLA ELAINE HALLWAY - DAY   225

     Robert ascends the stairs. As he enters the hallway he sees
     Seth pounding on one of the doors.

                         SETH
                    Open the door. Open the fucking door,
                    man.

     A MAN'S VOICE comes from the other side of the door.

                         MUFFLED VOICE
                    Go away!

     Robert closes the distance. Seth pounds harder.

                         SETH
                    I know she's in there. Let me talk to
                    her.

                         MUFFLED VOICE
                    I don't know what you're talking about.
                    Go away!

                                                        (CONTINUED)

225   CONTINUED: 225

Robert reaches the door. Seth sees him.

                    SETH
          I know she's in there.

Robert kicks the door in.

226   INT. HOTEL ROOM - DAY   226

Robert sees a middle-aged JOHN in his underwear and a dress
shirt.

                    JOHN
          Hey, I haven't touched her --

Caroline is passed out on the bed. Robert goes to her as the
John scrambles for his clothes.

She stirs and sees him --

                    CAROLINE
              (really out of it)
          Hi, Daddy.

227   INT. ROBERT'S CAR - DAY   227

Caroline rides in the passenger seat. She's come out of her
stupor and is now filled with ebullience.

                    CAROLINE
          It's gonna be great... I mean, I'm okay
          and all, because, see, I met a guy, he's
          in this pretty famous band and...
              (gets up confessional courage)
          They've invited me to write lyrics for
          them, I'm gonna be able to do that and
          maybe sing, too... not at first, but
          later.

Caroline gets lost in her grandiose vision. Robert looks over
at her as she drifts off into a nod. A moment later she's
awake and rambling again.

                    CAROLINE (cont'd)
              (sounding completely crazy)
          I've been doing research for the school
          paper, that's what I've been doing, like
          on assignment kind-of, I've seen some
          stuff you wouldn't believe, but I'm gonna
          write it all down into lyrics. They think
          I'm really good, everybody says so, what
          do you think?

                                                (CONTINUED)

Robert fights back tears. He reaches over and takes his
daughter's hand.

                                                              CUT TO:

228   OMITTED   228

229   OMITTED   229

230   OMITTED   230

231   OMITTED   231

232   OMITTED   232

233   OMITTED   233

234   OMITTED   234

235   OMITTED   235

A236   INT. CLUB PLATINUM OFFICE - DAY   A236

Juan Marquez sits across the desk from Javi. Tigrillo and
PABLO, 30's, are also in the meeting.

                         MARQUEZ
              Salazar and Madrigal are no longer with
              us.
                    (beat)
              A feat none of these people could get
              accomplished.

Juan nods toward Pablo and Tigrillo.

                         MARQUEZ (cont'd)
              You're going to be made the Special
              Assistant to the new drug Czar, which
              makes you a very valuable law enforcement
              officer.
                    (beat)
              I hope you like to travel because we have
              plans for Juarez and El Paso, Nogales,
              Sinaloa, Jalisco, Michoacan...

Javi just stares at him for a long moment, then looks off.

                                                              CUT TO:

236   INT. ROBERT'S OFFICE IN WASHINGTON - DAY   236

        Robert on the telephone.

                            ROBERT
                         (into phone)
                    How was she?

237   INT. BARBARA'S OFFICE - DAY   237

        A cramped, messy office at the Environmental Protection
        Agency. Barbara is on the phone.

                            BARBARA
                         (into phone)
                    I'm really not sure. She seemed to
                    recognize it wasn't Serenity Oaks. It's a
                    pretty hard-core facility, but at least
                    we know where she is.
                         (beat)
                    Maybe it's what she needs now.

A238   INTERCUT ROBERT IN HIS OFFICE   A238

        He holds the phone and doesn't say anything.

                                                        CUT TO:

238   INT. COURTROOM - EARLY MORNING   238

        The court is searched carefully by a phalanx of OFFICERS.
        Metal Detectors are checked. Bomb sniffing German Shepherds
        are led through the space.

239   INT. HOTEL SUITE - MORNING   239

        The agents are unkempt and everyone is tired. Ruiz moves
        through a cluttered room in a bathrobe with a cup of coffee.
        An agent shows him a morning paper --

                            AGENT
                    Big day.
                         (shows picture in paper)
                    You're a star.

        Ruiz walks over and sits across from Gordon, switching off
        the radio show he's listening to. Gordon looks up from his
        paper.

                            GORDON
                    Go shower. You smell.

        There is a KNOCK on the front door. An AGENT goes to answer --

                                                        (CONTINUED)

                              AGENT
                    Who is it?

                              SOMEBODY (V.O.)
                              (through the door)
                    The Mafia. I've got his breakfast.

The agent opens the door and is handed a breakfast tray. He
puts the food in front of Ruiz who uncovers the sausage and
eggs.

An agent walking by tries to take a bite of sausage. Ruiz
stabs it with a fork --

                              RUIZ
                    Fuck off.

Gordon watches the interchange --

                              GORDON
                    Where's the love gone, Eddie? You'll be
                    testifying for at least ten days. What if
                    we stop feeding you?

Ruiz begins to eat hungrily.

                              RUIZ
                    You expect me to be grateful for spending
                    the rest of my life looking over my
                    shoulder.

                              GORDON
                    That thought makes me feel awful.

Ruiz pushes eggs into a piece of toast.

                              RUIZ
                    Can't you for a second imagine none of
                    this had happened? That my drugs had gone
                    through. What would have been the harm? A
                    few people get high who are getting high
                    anyway. Your partner is still alive. We
                    avoid having breakfast together. Don't
                    you see this means nothing? That your
                    whole life is pointless?

                              GORDON
                    You're breaking my heart.

                              RUIZ
                    The worst thing about you, Monty, is you
                    realize the futility of what you're doing
                    and you do it anyway.
                              (MORE)

                              RUIZ (cont'd)
                    I wish you could see how transparent you
                    are.
                         (disgusted)
                    This food tastes like shit.

                              GORDON
                    So go shower already.

                              RUIZ
                    You only got to me because you were
                    tipped off by the Juarez Cartel, who's
                    trying to break into Tijuana. You're
                    helping them.
                         (beat)
                    You work for a drug dealer too, Monty.

Ruiz stands and heads for the bathroom.

                              GORDON
                         (yelling after him)
                    And shave. You better look nice and
                    believable for the jury.

Ruiz disappears into the bathroom and slams the door behind
him.

                              GORDON (cont'd)
                         (to another agent)
                    It's like having another wife.

The agent laughs. There's another KNOCK on the door.

                              GORDON (cont'd)
                    Who is it?

                              SOMEBODY ELSE (V.O.)
                         (through the door)
                    Breakfast.

Gordon and the agent look at each other.

                              SOMEBODY ELSE(V.O. Cont'd) (CONT'D)
                    Hurry up. It's getting cold.

Gordon moves to the side of the door and pulls his gun. The
other agent opens the door.

A MAN with a breakfast tray enters. Gordon puts the gun to
the side of his head.

                              MAN WITH TRAY
                    I'm on your side. God, you're jumpy.

                                                   (CONTINUED)

Gordon is momentarily confused, then goes for the bathroom door.

> GORDON
> Call an ambulance. Hurry.

Gordon tries the bathroom door. It's stuck. He gets it open a crack. There's a body against the other side. He shoves.

240   INT. BATHROOM - CONTINUOUS   240

Ruiz is on the floor in convulsions.

> GORDON
> (yelling)
> Call the ambulance.
> (to Ruiz)
> Don't die on me. You will not die on me.
> Do you hear me? Don't you die on me.

Ruiz's convulsions get worse, his claw-like fingers scratch across the tile.

                                                    CUT TO:

241   OMITTED   241

242   INT. COURTROOM - SAN DIEGO - DAY   242

The court is packed. Helena and Arnie watch from the gallery. The judge is at the bench.

The prosecutor rises --

> PROSECUTOR
> Your honor, ladies and gentlemen of the
> jury... Because of the sudden death of
> Eduardo Ruiz, the people have decided
> that at this point we cannot continue our
> case against Carl Ayala.

The court ERUPTS. Reporters scatter. Helena cheers.

                                                    CUT TO:

243   OMITTED   243

244   INT. WHITE HOUSE OFFICE - DAY   244

Robert Wakefield enters the office of the Chief of Staff, who looks up from what he's doing, which is reading Robert's report, and is already mid-sentence.

                                                    (CONTINUED)

244   CONTINUED: 244

                         CHIEF OF STAFF
                   Yeah, hi --
                         (waves Robert to a chair)
                   So I've got a copy of your speech here...
                         (glances down, still reading)
                   It's fantastic... So, Robert, my genuine
                   thanks. You're my choice and you're gonna
                   be great. The President is sorry he
                   hasn't been able to spend more time with
                   you. After the press conference he wants
                   to really sit down.
                         (an afterthought)
                   Oh, I got to the Post, too. Don't worry
                   about that thing with your daughter, it's
                   not news; they're willing to treat it as
                   a family matter, a personal matter.
                         (off Robert's stare)
                   Look, even if it came out, we'd turn it
                   into a qualification, *I've been in the
                   trenches of this Drug War, I have seen
                   the face of the enemy, etcetera.*

       Robert just stares at him.

                                                        CUT TO:

A245   INT. JAIL CELL - DAY   A245

       General Salazar sits in the same grimy cell that housed
       Francisco Flores. He is sweating and his breathing is
       labored. A DOCTOR enters and gives him an injection,
       explaining that it will calm him down.

245   EXT. DESERT OUTSIDE TIJUANA - DAY   245

       It's a reprise of the earlier desert bust... a landing strip
       in the middle of nowhere, a plane landing, SUV's approaching.

       This time Javi is at the wheel of one of them. News crews are
       trailing behind him.

246   EXT. DESERT AIRSTRIP - LATER   246

       Javi and Special Agent Hughes stand next to a giant mound of
       seized cocaine, the same cocaine, in fact, Javi held briefly
       at the beginning. The same teenagers from the pickup truck
       have been arrested. The news crews get everything.

                         JAVIER
                         (to the press)
                   This seizure is one of the largest
                   seizures in Mexican history...
                         (MORE)

                                                   (CONTINUED)

                         JAVIER (cont'd)
                    It represents the first bilateral effort
                    of the American DEA and the Mexican
                    I.N.C.D.

A247 INT. JAIL CELL - DAY   A247

     General Salazar lies on his side, eyes and mouth open. He is
     dead. Javier looks at him through the doorway.

                         JAVIER (V.O. CONT'D)
                    Today I'm very proud to announce that
                    Mexico, with the help of our American
                    partners, is finally winning the war
                    against narcotics trafficking.

     The PRESS begins shouting questions --

                                                          CUT TO:

247 OMITTED   247

248 INT. HEADQUARTERS, I.N.C.D. - MEXICO - DAY   248

     Robert and Javi walk through the headquarters, a nondescript
     government building.

     Robert extracts photographs of the bust from a manila
     envelope. The crates of cocaine are clearly marked "911."

                         ROBERT
                    The cocaine brand, *911,* is an East Coast
                    brand, a Juarez Cartel brand, and you
                    must know it usually comes through into
                    El Paso?

                         JAVIER
                    I'm aware of that.

                         ROBERT
                    So what's it doing in Tijuana?

     Javi looks Robert Wakefield squarely in the eye. He shrugs.

                         ROBERT (cont'd)
                    Let me ask you a hypothetical question:
                    if Salazar worked for Madrigal and the
                    Juarez cartel, and he went out of power,
                    would it mean the Juarez Cartel is losing
                    influence?

                         JAVIER
                    It could mean that, yes.

                                                     (CONTINUED)

>   ROBERT
>   That would probably mean the Tijuana
>   Cartel is gaining power?

>   JAVIER
>   It's possible.

>   ROBERT
>   Is it possible to have a Drug Czar in
>   Mexico who isn't connected in some way to
>   one of the cartels?

Javi thinks along time before answering.

>   JAVIER
>   Yeah, it's possible... if you're prepared
>   to die.

                                                            CUT TO:

249 EXT. AYALA FRONT YARD - AFTERNOON   249

An outdoor party is going on. Children and adults arrive and
mingle. Caterers work the barbecue grill. Waiters serve food
and drink on the rolling lawn.

Helena circles through the crowd greeting friends. She looks
past her tree line and up the street where a telephone repair
van is parked. She turns back toward her guests. Somebody has
raised a cup and everyone is CHEERING.

Helena drinks with her guests, then walks inside her house.

AT THE FRONT GATE

Montel Gordon walks through the gate and up the drive. He
grabs a drink off the tray of a passing waiter. He appears
drunk.

Montel follows Helena into the house.

250 INT. CARL'S PRIVATE STUDY - AFTERNOON   250

Carl hears the CHEERING outside and the sound of LAUGHTER. He
makes a cellular telephone call.

251 INT. ARNIE METZGER'S OFFICE - AFTERNOON   251

Arnie is in his office and answers the cell phone --

>   CARLOS (V.O.)
>   It's Saturday, Arnie. You work too hard.

                                                      (CONTINUED)

                          ARNIE
               Carl, I'm running late. I'm coming right
               now --

Behind Arnie in the office there is a movement of SHADOW.

252 INT. CARL'S PRIVATE STUDY - AFTERNOON   252

     Carl stands at the window looking at his guests while he
     talks on the phone --

                          CARLOS
               Don't bother.

                          ARNIE (V.O.)
               What?

                          CARLOS
               So Arnie, when were you going to tell me
               about the 3 million dollars we got in
               from San Francisco two days after I got
               arrested?

                          ARNIE (V.O.)
               I was just waiting for the right time.

                          CARLOS
               And you didn't feel like you could trust
               my wife with this news?

                          ARNIE (V.O.)
               I just didn't want to take a chance. I
               didn't want to risk it. It could have
               been frozen along with everything else.

                          CARLOS
               You had it all figured out. You move into
               my house. You raise my kids. You sleep
               with my wife. It was a good plan, Arnie.

                          ARNIE (V.O.)
               Carl, that's insane.

                          CARLOS
               So my wife is lying?

                          ARNIE (V.O.)
               Carl, think about it, if I was trying to
               rip you off, I would have left town after
               Ruiz was killed. I wouldn't sit next to
               you in court listening to the dismissal.

                                                    (CONTINUED)

252 CONTINUED: 252

On the front lawn CHILDREN are lined up for the ice-cream
sundae bar that is being tended by a WAITER.

> CARLOS
> Arnie, do think there's a difference
> between a reason and an excuse, because I
> don't think there is.

> ARNIE (V.O.)
> Carl --

> CARLOS
> Goodbye, Arnie.

253   INT. ARNIE METZGER'S OFFICE - AFTERNOON   253

Arnie turns around and there are TWO MEN in his office.

254   INT. CARL'S PRIVATE STUDY - AFTERNOON   254

Carl hears MUFFLED GUNSHOTS over the phone. He hangs up and
turns from the window. Helena is standing there.

> HELENA
> Who was that?

> CARLOS
> Arnie. He's not going to be able to make
> the barbecue.

Carl and Helena share an embrace and a kiss.

> HELENA
> Come downstairs. Everyone is waiting.

Carl and Helena turn to leave the room and Montel Gordon is
standing in the doorway with his glass of champagne.

> GORDON
> Hello, Helena. What a great party.

> CARLOS
> Who are you?

> GORDON
> Nobody. I'm a nobody who arrested you,
> but your wife is a murderer.

Gordon takes a sip of his drink. Two SECURITY OFFICERS appear
in the doorway behind him.

> SECURITY OFFICER
> Hey, you can't be in here.

(CONTINUED)

                    GORDON
          I'm a cop.

                    SECURITY OFFICER
          I don't care.

                    HELENA
                  (to the guards)
          Throw him out of here.

The security officers grab Gordon. There is a scuffle. Gordon
falls to the floor by the window. They are wrestling. As they
wrestle, Gordon reaches out and, unnoticed, affixes a TINY
LISTENING DEVICE underneath the desk.

He continues to struggle with the guards. Helena and Carlos
start from the room.

                    GORDON
                  (calling out)
          You didn't win, Helena. You lost
          everything. Tell your children a nice
          bedtime story... How you killed my
          partner.

255   EXT. AYALA FRONT YARD - AFTERNOON   255

The guests watch as the guards eject Gordon from the
premises.

Near the gate David has stopped playing to watch the action.

Then he goes back to playing with his toy: a Spastic Jack
figure.

                                                          CUT TO:

256   EXT. VERDANT NEIGHBORHOOD - MEXICO CITY - DAY   256

Javi and his convoy of armored SUV's pull up in front of the
beautiful house where earlier he deposited Rosario, Salazar's
former mistress.

Javier opens the front door and Rosario greets him by
throwing her arms around his neck. They disappear inside.

                                                          CUT TO:

257   INT. WHITE HOUSE PRESS ROOM - DAY   257

The PRESS SECRETARY stands at the familiar podium addressing
the White House Press Corps.

                                                      (CONTINUED)

Robert Wakefield stands to one side with the Chief of Staff,
his lawyers, Sheridan and General Landry.

                    PRESS SECRETARY
               ... a sterling reputation and close
               friend of the President, recently
               confirmed into The Office of National
               Drug Control Policy... our new Drug Czar,
               Robert Hudson Wakefield.

Applause from the assembled PRESS. The Press Secretary
signals and Robert walks to the podium. He looks back to the
Chief of Staff; he stares out at the expectant faces and
television lights and camera flashes.

                    ROBERT
               (reading his prepared speech)
               The War on Drugs is a war on our nation's
               most precious resource... our children.
               Sixty-eight million children have been
               targeted by those who perpetrate this war
               and protecting those children must be
               priority number one.
                    (beat)
               There has been progress and there have
               been failures, but where we have fallen
               short I see not a problem but an
               opportunity.

Robert is becoming increasingly uneasy. He glances at the
Chief of Staff who bores into him. He looks again at his
speech. With great effort he continues.

                    ROBERT (cont'd)
               An opportunity to correct the mistakes of
               the past while laying a solid foundation
               for the future.
                    (a long, uncomfortable beat)
               This takes not only new ideas, but
               perseverance. This takes not only
               resources, but courage. This takes not
               only government, but families.

Robert stops again as though the words are choking him.

                    ROBERT (cont'd)
               I've... I've outlined a ten-point plan,
               representing a new bilateral effort...

He can't finish. Everyone stares at Robert. The crowd of
reporters senses something is wrong.

                                                         (CONTINUED)

                         ROBERT (cont'd)
              I can't do this.
                   (beat)
              If there is a War on Drugs then our own
              families have become the enemy. How can
              you wage war on your own family?

He walks out of the room. The crowd waits, expecting him to
return.

Robert walks down a corridor and out of the White House.

258 EXT. WHITE HOUSE - DAY   258

A beautiful spring morning. He walks down to Pennsylvania
Avenue. He hails a cab and gets in. The cab pulls away.

259 INT. CHURCH BASEMENT - DAY   259

A twelve step meeting is in progress. Caroline shares from
her seat.

                         CAROLINE
              On the good days I feel like I get it,
              like it all makes sense. I can stay in
              the moment. I don't have to control
              everything in the future. And I believe
              everything is going to work out fine.
                   (beat)
              On the bad days, I just want to grab the
              phone and start dialing numbers. I want
              to pull my hair and run through the
              streets screaming.
                   (beat)
              But, thanks to the people I've met in
              these rooms, people like Margaret and Jim
              and Sarah, people who've taught me how to
              listen, I'm pretty sure I'll make it
              through today.

Caroline is finished sharing.

                         VOICE (O.S.)
              Would you like to share?

We pan over to reveal Robert and Barbara sitting next to
Caroline.

                                                    (CONTINUED)

259 CONTINUED: 259

                              ROBERT
                    My name is Robert. This is my wife,
                    Barbara. We're Caroline's parents. We're
                    just hear to listen.

                                                        CUT TO:

260 OMIT.   260

261 EXT. AYALA HOME - NIGHT   261

     The house is dark and silent. The van is parked up the
     street.

262 INT. VAN - NIGHT   262

     Gordon listens through a headset, his expression set.

                              CARLOS (V.O.)
                         (over a listening device)
                    We're back up and running. Completely
                    untouchable. Completely.

                                                        CUT TO:

263 EXT. BASEBALL FIELD - TIJUANA - NIGHT   263

     A bank of lights CRANKS on. Then ANOTHER and ANOTHER.

     In a wider shot we see an illuminated baseball field where a
     children's pickup game is in progress.

     In the crowd, Javi serenely watches the game.

                              THE END

STILLS

MICHAEL DOUGLAS
as Robert Wakefield

CATHERINE ZETA-JONES
as Helena Ayala

BENICIO DEL TORO
as Javier Rodriguez

DON CHEADLE
as Montel Gordon

LUIS GUZMAN
as Ray Castro

DENNIS QUAID
as Arnie Metzger

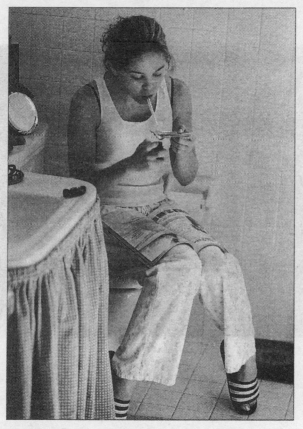

ERIKA CHRISTENSEN
as Caroline Wakefield

ALBERT FINNEY
as Chief of Staff

BENJAMIN BRATT
as Juan Obregón

JAMES BROLIN
as General Ralph Landry

Top: Scene 79: Caroline Wakefield spends the night in a juvenile detention center.
Bottom: Scene A57: Javier Rodriguez and Manolo Sanchez wait to meet General Salazar.

Top: Scene 140: Robert Wakefield discovers Caroline using drugs. *Bottom:* Scene 129: Arnie Metzger and Helena Ayala discuss Carl's situation.